Stop Overthinking

Evidence-Based Tips and Techniques to
Conquer Negative Thoughts, Manage Anxiety
and Quickly Calm the Mind

Linda Hill

Linda Hill

Table of Contents

Linda Hill

Your Free Gift

As a way of saying thanks for your purchase, I want to offer you a free bonus e-Book called How to Say "No", exclusive to readers of this book.

In this book you'll discover:

- How to say "no" without feeling guilty or hurting other's feelings

- How to quit people pleasing and stand up for yourself

- How to distinguish between being a helpful person and being a doormat

- And so much more

If you finally want to end people pleasing for good, then grab this book.

To get instant access, just go to:

PeakPublishBooks.com/people

Or Scan the QR Code below:

Introduction

Overthinking is a silent crippler. It sneaks into your brain unnoticeably, and it latches and holds onto you for what feels like forever. So how does it even get in? Simply put, it starts because we worry about something. While that may be a gross oversimplification to some people, for this book, that will suffice as a general understanding of how it appears like you have become an overthinker seemingly overnight.

In truth, overthinking is often—but not always—latched onto a deeper mental condition such as depression, anxiety, eating disorders, or substance use disorders; but, that is not always the case. The problem is that the correlation between overthinking and those other conditions become a chicken and egg scenario. It is not entirely clear which came first and started the other until you deep dive with licensed professionals (Morin, 2020).

Just because overthinking is often linked to the above mental conditions does not mean that they always occur together; there are multiple other reasons that any of these conditions can occur, but it is good to mention them now, so that you can begin to create self-awareness.

Understanding Overthinking

The problem with overthinking is that because it is so prevalent in our lives, many people either dismiss their overthinking tendencies, or begin to develop an overthinking complex about overthinking. While this book is going to go more in-depth on how to identify your personal overthinking triggers and patterns, we are going to begin with a generalized understanding of overthinking and how it works.

What is Overthinking

The definition of overthinking is as follows: "To think too much about (something): to put too much time into thinking about or analyzing (something) in a way that is more harmful than helpful" (Merriam-Webster, n.d.). Before going any further into understanding overthinking, there is something very important in the definition which must be pointed out: Overthinking becomes dangerous when we think to the point that our thoughts become more harmful than helpful.

Another great way to look at it is to see that overthinking is very closely associated with worry or rumination; especially since those two actions can easily be justified as trying to do something beneficial or productive. For example, we explain to ourselves, friends, family members, and co-workers that we are worrying about someone's health, or that we are preparing ourselves for the worst outcome (Acosta, 2022). In actuality, we are mentally preparing for every worst-case scenario, and are really making things worse for ourselves in the long run.

By giving ourselves the conscious belief that we are doing something positive or productive through worrying, or engaging in ruminating thoughts, we allow those types of thoughts and behaviors to continue. The problem is that allowing ourselves to continue thinking this way actually encourages our brain to persist in the ingrained subconscious negative thinking patterns those types of thoughts induce.

Now, before going any further, we must acknowledge the elephant in the room. Yes, the above paragraphs make it seem like you, as an overthinker, are openly welcoming that type of thinking, into your mind with open arms. This book is not saying that. While you are technically in control over what thoughts you allow, overthinking is a habit, and it tends to begin associating anxious, obsessive, ruminative, depressive feelings—or any other type of associated negative feelings—to your original thoughts, without you even noticing. It is a sad fact, but most overthinkers are not even completely aware they overthink, or of the extent that their brain goes to while in that state. Which is why this book opened with the statement that overthinking is so pervasive and sneaky, and that most people perpetuate the cycle without even noticing it. If this is you, there is absolutely nothing to be ashamed of or upset over. A lot of us have engaged in over thinking at one point in time.

We all overthink sometimes. However, the key difference between an overthinker—where that type of thinking has become a way of life and way to create safety—compared to others, is what is done with the reasons behind overthinking. A non-overthinker will use specific scenarios where overthinking is necessary to create a positive outcome or to meet a requirement. Examples of this could be a project at work or finally coming up with a way to have a confrontation with someone close to them. However, overthinkers tend to use the exact same thought patterns to continue cycles of negativity, worrying, and self-loathing.

Essentially, if your overthinking phase has a pre-set end date (like a project due date or the day of that coffee with someone), and you are able to not overthink the scenario too much after the event then you are most likely not an overthinker. (It is completely normal, however, to go over a traumatic event for a few hours or days after the actual event, because you need time to process it.) True overthinkers fixate on anything and everything, and there really is no end date as to when that stops.

Why might that type of thinking have no end date? The answer to that could honestly be almost anything. It could be because your brain is wired this way (this will be discussed as we progress), it could be that something about your previous overthinking triggered something in your brain to keep it going, or it could be that the time you needed to overthink caused your brain to regress back to old ways of thinking. Sadly, overthinking is one of those things where it just pops up, and there could be many reasons as to why it has. Try to not let that dishearten you. While you may be an overthinker, or you may know someone who is, there are plenty of ways to fight it, and we will discuss many of those in this book. So, let's keep going.

How Overthinking Works

There are two main types of overthinking: worrying about the past, or worrying about the future (Morrin,

2019). Since these two ways of thinking are common in modern society, it makes sense that so many people ignore their overthinking tendencies. On top of that, the increased 'normal' levels of stress most of us now experience begin to alter our brains chemically, in the ways we think, and the actual size and abilities of our brains, which in turn enables overthinking to become a stronger habit (TED-Ed, 2015).

What Overthinking Is Not

Alright, so now that you have the definition of overthinking, and how it manifests, it is important that you understand what overthinking is *not*. Since overthinking latches onto thinking, is triggered by multiple unknown variables, and can even persist in your brain without your full awareness, let's just make sure that you fully understand what is happening, rather than worrying about every type of in-depth thinking we go through as humans. We are going to quickly run through a list of what overthinking is not, and why these types of thinking is not overthinking.

Problem Solving

Problem solving is an intensive form of thinking. It involves looking at every possible scenario to find the best solution and outcome. The main difference between problem solving and overthinking is that when you are problem solving, you are focused on finding a solution. In comparison, overthinking dwells on the problem, and never really finds a solution that is actually usable (Morrin, 2019).

Self-Reflection

While self-reflection can also cause negative mental spirals, the main difference between self-reflection and overthinking is that with healthy self-reflection, you are learning something about yourself (Morrin, 2019). In comparison, overthinking tends to dwell on anything and everything that is wrong with you, and will even come up with things that are not wrong, but that you now believe are wrong.

If that sounds a bit odd, think about a time when someone you know was down on themselves and believed something which was completely wrong about who and what they were, and what they could do. That right there is a form of overthinking. We somehow end up believing negative things about ourselves that no one else does.

Your Brain and Emotions

Okay, so now that overthinking has been given a good rudimentary understanding, it is time to look at your brain and emotions. Why? Because overthinking is emotionally based, and when our emotions are involved, it is helpful to understand the science behind them in order to completely understand what is happening to us

The Basics

As mentioned earlier, stress goes hand-in-hand with overthinking; and, it really does not matter where your stress comes from. Whether we overthink because we are stressed, or our stress comes from overthinking, it is still there. What stress does to your brain is particularly important to understand.

Now, before we make stress the ultimate villain, I need to be clear that it is not. Bursts of stress can be great for competitive or high-adrenaline events like sports, or help you possibly perform better at work or in school. The thing is, in order for that to happen, you have to be able to mentally handle your stress correctly. While this book will have a few ways on how to do that in an upcoming chapter, the ways we will discuss how to combat stress in this chapter will predominantly deal with overthinking rather than your overall life.

So, back to how stress impacts you. Chronic stress, such as constant arguments or a toxic work environment can actually affect the size, functionality, and even the most basic level of your genes within the brain. When your brain recognizes stress, it releases a chemical called cortisol, which gives your body that boost of energy to instantly take action in the situation. The problem is that high levels of cortisol over long periods of time will hurt your brain. It will stop your brain's fear center as well as the parts of your brain that help with learning, socializing, and controlling stress. Additionally, cortisol can cause your brain to shrink in size, specifically through a loss in brain synapses, and a reduction in these brain cells being made throughout the brain's regular functions (TED-Ed, 2015).

Overall, the constant presence of cortisol long term is very damaging, and opens your brain up to numerous potential problems such as anxiety and depression.

Going Deeper

So then, how does your brain affect your overthinking? Well, there are numerous ways it does that, but for the purposes of this book, we are going to focus mainly on the thoughts, rather than the chemical imbalances.

Thanks to Dr. Carolyn Leaf and her peers, this topic has begun to be broken down into more easily understandable pieces, the first of which is that your brain and your mind are actually two completely separate entities residing in the same 'area' (your brain). Our thoughts are the very first thing that happens before anything else, and they occur in our minds. If we want to change, we have to change our thoughts. Think about it. If you want to lose weight, you have to actually come up with that thought in your mind. Our minds are where we react and respond to life around us. Since our mind is separate from our brain, what our mind decides directly influences our brain and how it functions.

Your mind thinks, and your brain reacts and responds.

Thoughts vs Memories

Our thoughts are the product of how our minds respond to our lives while we are asleep. Our thoughts are actual physical things inside of our brains. If you ever remember seeing tree-like structures when discussing brains and neural pathways, thoughts are those trees. They are your thoughts, and the emotions tied to them. Consider a tree and what it is made of. Our memories are the roots of the trees inside our brains. Our thoughts themselves are what created that tree, and as the moment passes, the tree becomes inhabited by a memory of that thought. Every one of these thought trees can have hundreds of memories inside of them. What is that tree rooted to? Your brain. Which means that you are literally building into your brain the responses of your mind which come from your experiences, words, feelings, choices, and responses. This is how we begin to function, create good memories, and also how we create trauma within our brains.

A thought is made up of memories. Think of a photo album. The thought is the event being photographed, and the memories are the photographs.

All right, this is now the incredibly important bit for this book: The events in our environment are neurally encoded into our brains and bodies, and we know this thanks to psychoneurobiology. Therefore, whatever we constantly think about creates a stronger encoding on that particular thought and its associated emotions. In simpler terms, whatever we think about the most, grows. And as many of us know, what we think, feel, and choose, begins to dictate what we say, do, and even how we approach life. Therefore, when we constantly think about negative things, or think using negative thought patterns—like overthinking—we are building negativity into our brains (Leaf, 2019).

Breathe

Alright, that was a lot to get through, and a lot of very big facts thrown your way. Since this book is about overthinking, that was potentially a lot of new information to give your most-likely cortisol-happy brain to now begin turning over repeatedly.

First: Just because this is what is happening when you are overthinking does not mean this is what is happening now, or that your brain is always this way. The previous section merely mentions what happens when your brain is exposed to too much cortisol over long periods of time.

Second: Your brain is able to bounce back. Thanks to numerous wonderful studies and professionals who have done quite a bit of research, we know that when you put in the hard work, your brain is able to heal and fix itself (TEDx Talks, 2020a). However, it should be noted that while our brains can change and adapt, there also comes a very strong argument on the type of environment you are constantly putting your brain into. Your brain is adaptable and is wired for change, but it cannot change when it is fighting every type of environmental factor possible (there are maybe a few people among thousands of others who have this mental strength). Therefore, start to be mindful of the environments you are putting yourself into. If your surrounding environment is always negative, you are going to have a very hard time remaining and staying positive (TEDx Talks, 2020b). If you want your brain to overcome overthinking and adapt to a new normal, then you are going to have to begin to set yourself up for success.

Before Continuing

Before going further into overthinking, there are a few other things you should know and do while reading this book. It is heavily advised that you read and consider these things before continuing.

Terms

Some terms in this book may not be familiar to a few of you. In case that happens, they will be explained in this section. Many of these terms and ideas can be used in areas of your life outside of overthinking, so if you see something that you can use in another area, go ahead and do that!

Safe People

Safe people are the people in our lives who we can tell absolutely anything to and they will never judge us, harm us, or guilt us into changing our mind. They may encourage us to make better or different choices, but they respect us as a human and foster personal, professional, and relational growth (Cloud & John Sims Townsend, 2022/2016). These are the types of people who will never judge us and it is one of the healthiest relationships you have.

It is strongly recommended that for certain aspects of this journey, you ask one of your safe people to come alongside you and help you work through certain things. A bonus of using a safe person over a licensed therapist is that they have most likely known you a long time, and can add clarity and insight where your memories are not exactly the most reliable.

There will be many times in this book where your safe people will be mentioned, and you may even be encouraged to talk to them. However, be sure to make your safe person aware of what they are agreeing to. It is not fair, or necessarily kind, to make your safe person an accountability partner, or to bring them on this journey if they are unaware of that. Additionally, it would cause them to not give you the best advice.

If You Do Not Have a Safe Person

Sadly, there are times in our lives where safe people are not easily accessible, or those relationships are no longer as strong as they once were. If that is the case, find a professional therapist or licensed counselor for those times when you need help. These are the only type of people who can be safe right away, because they are professionally trained and most likely have quite a few other clients with similar problems.

Do not make someone you just met a safe person. While there is the potential for that down the road, the reason safe people are safe is because you have spent time getting to know them and building that relationship. Additionally, a new person may not be aware of how much you overthink, and what is more, they may not know enough of you as a person and your personal history to give you the best advice.

Accountability Partner

Similar to safe people, accountability partners are people who hold us accountable for certain things in our lives. This can be to stop us from continuing a negative pattern or to help us through an addiction. For this book, accountability partners will be used as a safeguard to ensure that you begin implementing the steps needed to stop overthinking; or, to encourage you as you scale up some of the practices you pick from this book.

When picking an accountability partner, you need to find someone you will listen to. Someone who can get into your face, get in touch with you to check up on you, and who you trust. You will also need to be prepared for what your accountability partner brings to the table. You need to be okay with the fact that they will get in your face, call you out, and ask for updates. You will also need to be honest with them. Lying to an accountability partner is like wearing a snowsuit in the desert it will do you absolutely no good. If your accountability partner makes you feel less than, or you do not feel comfortable sharing your failures with them because of their behaviors or reactions, find a different accountability partner.

Additionally, just like with safe people, these people need to be aware that they are your accountability partner so that they can fulfill that role. An accountability partner who is unaware that that is their role will do you no good in ensuring you are maintaining the steps for the habits when things get hard, or when you have a bad day.

Boundaries

According to Dr. Henry Cloud, boundaries are recognizing what we are, or are not, willing to be responsible for in our own lives (Cloud & John Sims Townsend, 2022/2004). This is especially important in overthinking, as it is beginning to build the mental and emotional awareness of when your thoughts are beginning to put more responsibility on you than you need, or should be accountable for in that particular scenario.

When you are having trouble thinking about if something is actually your responsibility, begin to relate that situation to an item of clothing, or to your house.

We all know what we are or are not responsible for when it comes to material things. For instance, think about homeowners. Homeowners are very well-versed on what is their responsibility compared to other people such as their neighbors or municipal governments; and they have the tendency to not bend on those responsibilities. Similarly, most people are perfectly aware of what they own or want to add to their closet. Simply begin to ask yourself what you are willing to be and should be responsible for here in a given situation. If you need another incentive to start setting boundaries for yourself, knowing your boundaries is a great way to begin combatting overthinking, because it forces your brain and emotions to recognize what is your problem, and what is not.

Small Note

The 'should' in that above statement is in regards to personal responsibilities, and not what someone else is putting onto you. For instance, if you are responsible for managing the team meetings at work, your boundary cannot directly go against that (unless there is a dangerous and unhealthy situation), because that is what you agreed to when you took on that position (if it is not, then you should talk to your boss). In comparison, say your partner or friend is mad that you went to a different restaurant than what they wanted, but they did not speak up about their preference, when asked.

Between the two examples, one is clearly showing a responsibility that you have whether you want it or not, versus a situation where someone put a responsibility onto you that was never yours to begin with (to read their mind and know which restaurant they wanted to go to). Overthinking tends to fall into the second category, except you are the one who puts more of the responsibility onto yourself. Beginning to recognize when you do that will be incredibly beneficial throughout the rest of this book.

Toxic Positivity

Toxic positivity is a bit of a new term, which can sadly be overgeneralized to the point where it sounds like being positive is toxic. That is not what this term means. Toxic positivity is essentially the act of belittling your emotions or a negative scenario in order to remain positive. It is all well and good to use positivity to cheer yourself or others up, but it should not be done at the cost of someone's emotions or neglecting to honor their scenarios (Cherry, 2021).

There are tons of great resources and examples of showing the difference between toxic positivity and actually encouraging and helping someone, but for now, we will go through one brief example. For instance, instead of generalizing and saying, "It will be fine," you can specifically ask, "How can I help you?" In this example, the sentiments are the same, since the first one was most likely said with the underlying intent of trying to cheer someone up and be helpful, but the second example explicitly acknowledges that the person you are talking to needs help and you are willing to provide some.

It may seem small and trivial, but directly acknowledging someone's pain and problems—even though it may feel awkward—sometimes be all the person needs. Especially in regards to overthinking. As overthinkers, we tend to overgeneralize and belittle our own feelings and emotions—or over exaggerate them—to the point where we know we need help, but are unwilling to ask. Then, when faced with toxic positivity in the form where we actually feel like our feelings are being ignored, we shut down and do not attempt to continue asking for help.

Journaling

Journaling, whether it be on a notepad, document, or recorded voice memo, is a great way to begin gaining perspective on things you notice, are concerned about, or even just beginning to recognize as important self-reflection moments. This habit will also be incredibly beneficial while reading this book, as it will help you begin to gain perspective and really narrow down your overthinking habits and what you personally will need to focus on.

The chapters within this book will each have a journaling section where you will be encouraged to begin thinking about what you have read and how it directly correlates to you. When you are answering and thinking about these questions, there are several things you need to remember. First, these journals are meant to be the big picture of your life, its events, and your thoughts, feelings, and introspections. Meaning, it is completely okay to go on a long tangent and forget what you were saying, or to bring up an old painful memory. Sometimes, spilling our hearts out onto a piece of paper, including those weird mental tangents, helps bring us a clarity we would never achieve otherwise. So go for it. Second, these journaling moments are going to bring out many introspective moments. Meaning, you are going to have to take long and hard looks at your own emotions and the 'why' behind them. You may not always fully get the 'why,' but even beginning to think that way will help you begin to get to the point of where and how overthinking rooted itself into your daily life.

Be Honest

When it comes to overthinking, we may not always be sure what is the actual truth, since our brains have most likely muddled everything to the point where nothing is clear, and we feel like we are floating above ground. When it comes to journaling, or any other part of this process, you need to be honest with yourself about where you are in your overthinking process. Lying to yourself, ignoring warning signs in your brain, or pushing through those feelings, will not be helpful. There is a difference between perseverance and ignoring a clear warning sign. Remember, no one has to see this journal, and no one really should (unless you want to share it). So let the ugly truth out, because if you are not honest even in your own journal, you are never going to be honest with yourself, and a lot of the prompts and helpful ideas and suggestions in this book will be of no help. This includes allowing yourself to feel and express certain emotions, even if you know they are disproportionate to the scenario or that you cannot fully understand why you are feeling a certain way.

It may take awhile for you to begin differentiating between these things while overthinking in the beginning. Be honest about even that. If you are not honest to yourself about this journey, then you are allowing another loophole to exist that your overthinking brain might take advantage of.

While it is painful, messy, and sometimes brings up things we wish we did not have to admit about ourselves, honesty and determination are the key to change. You already have the determination, because you are reading this book. It is the honesty bit that may be a bit more challenging, but you can do it.

Be Human

It might sound strange, but prepare yourself to be okay being human. This means that certain portions of this book may be messy, will not be fun, and you may encounter parts of yourself or ways of thinking that you do not like. You do not have to like any of it, but you do have to embrace it and use those traits to propel yourself forward. Allowing yourself to be human will hopefully be the open door you need to begin encouraging that mindset and concession in regards to the standards you normally hold yourself to.

This Will Be a Journey

While it may not need to be said, since this book is about overthinking, it is worth the gamble to remind you: This journey will be worth it, and you are not alone. Overthinking is sadly quite common, especially in younger generations. Do not let the overthinking and negative mental pathways convince you that you are alone. You are not. You can do this, and you are completely able to do this. You may not succeed right away, and you may need to try and restart several times. But the journey will be worth it.

Get Help

Do not be afraid to get professional help if you think you need it. There is nothing to be ashamed of in admitting that you need someone who can constantly be in your life to help you, and paying a licensed therapist or counselor is a safe way to do it.

Whatever way you decide to continue on this journey, there is no shame in what you did, and you can change it to meet your needs.

CHAPTER 1

Overthinking Is the Root of It All

This may sound almost too simplistic for how intensive this book is about to become (if it has not hit that point already), but overthinking is most likely the root of many problems in your life. Even ones you have not considered yet.

For instance, have your friends and family, or partner, been saying that you are not being present, or you have been putting off having discussions with them? Have you been meaning to do certain things—which really should not take long for you to do—but they seem to never get done?

There are plenty of small, seemingly harmless examples like those above which may actually be a product of you overthinking; a form of paralysis. (Or, you could just be a procrastinator, or have many other logical reasons as to why those things have not happened.)

However, you did buy this book.

In case you are unsure, or you want concrete examples of what overthinking might look like, this chapter will cover exactly that. We will go through what thinking about thinking is, how it relates to overthinking, and then begin to go through several symptoms and causes of being an overthinker.

Thinking About Thinking

It may sound a bit odd, but thinking about thinking is a great way to know if you are an overthinker. Let's break that down a bit. When it comes to overthinking, thinking about thinking looks like you are obsessing and overanalyzing your thoughts constantly. It might even be at the point where you are doing this subconsciously in non-stressful situations. It has become a habit. One that is actually quite exhausting and not at all good for your brain, your emotions, or you in the long run.

What's worse, thinking about thinking could look harmless or even be guised as being productive, because you are thinking about your thoughts and how you are going about those thoughts. Yet the main difference between an overthinker who is thinking about thinking, and someone who is actually attempting to build more awareness about their thoughts, is what they do with it (which is going to become a common trend in comparing overthinkers to non-overthinkers). For instance, an overthinker will use thinking about thinking to continue a negative cycle and begin to actually create obsessive thoughts about their thinking. In comparison, a non-overthinker who is thinking about thinking is consciously being aware of their thoughts to be able to change habits they have accidentally created.

Consider the following example:

Amy is having a stressful day at work and ended up having a pretty heated conversation with her friend,

Anne. While the conflict was resolved, Amy began to replay that conversation over and over in her head throughout the rest of the week, and began to doubt her choices, words, and even her friendship with Anne, even though they had resolved the conflict the same day.

In comparison, Anne took a look at her conflict with Amy and began to break down their conversation to see where she could have handled things better. Anne was able to responsibly admit what was her fault, what she could have done better, and what was not her fault in the entire scenario. Anne began to identify and think about where she could improve her interpersonal skills and started to create habits to change those reactions for future conflicts.

Amy used her thinking about thinking to begin a negative cycle about herself and her relationship, which in turn, contributed to her overthinking habit. In comparison, Anne used thinking about thinking to bring hindsight and clarity to where she could improve her relationship with Amy going forward.

What Anne did in the example is called 'metacognition,'

which is the art of regulating and changing your thoughts and actions to consciously create a form of heightened self-awareness. While metacognition is actually one of the end-goals of this book, it is not what overthinkers generally gravitate towards while overthinking. Overthinkers use thinking about thinking to constantly obsess and over analyze their thoughts and actions to the point where they begin to create self-doubt, worry, anxiety, and maybe even depression.

If you do this, do not worry. We will go over other signs and manifestations of overthinking, but bringing up thinking about thinking was really the hook to get some of you who were unsure about whether you were actually an overthinker or not to begin questioning some of your mental habits and responses.

Signs You Are an Overthinker

In this section, we will discuss the signs of an overthinker as well as give examples on how these types of thinking and actions can present themselves. Each section will also contain examples of non-overthinkers, to help gain perspective on where overthinking begins to take over a relatively normal way of thinking.

Obsessive and Anxious Thoughts

When you are in a stressful situation, like a work project, deciding to end a relationship, or preparing for a confrontation with someone close to you, it is perfectly normal, natural, and healthy to obsess and be anxious over it—as long as those thoughts are within the immediate lead-up and aftermath of that particular scenario.

Why is this healthy? Because first of all it is for a short period of time. The before and after, if you will. During those times you are preparing yourself and then de-escalating your after-rush of endorphins in direct response to a relatively traumatic or stressful situation. Whether you actually are or not, your brain is mentally preparing you to go to war. You need all those hyped-up emotions to get through it and survive after the event.

The problem is when these obsessive and anxious

thoughts are in no way related to an immediate trigger for stress. Perhaps you constantly go over one particular conversation or scenario, or perhaps you are always anxious about what could happen, what people think, or what you have done. Another way to look at it is if you are constantly worrying.

Worrying in and of itself is a relatively common enough mental state, unfortunately; however, there is a time and place to worry. For example, if you are in the hospital or you are going into a serious meeting. Those are definitely times in your life when you should worry. Even low-key worrying about if your partner's parents will like you, or even just meeting someone new in general, is normal and natural.

Being obsessive and anxious about your thoughts and worries, however, is not. What makes it worse is that oftentimes we use these worry cycles and obsessive and anxious thoughts as a mental 'relief.' We believe that if we think about these things enough, we will be able to prepare ourselves for what is to come, and in turn, somehow magically prevent our worrying and anxiety about the uncertain future (Stein, n.d.). The problem is that the solution our brains have come up with actually encourages the types of thoughts which make our worries worse.

That may have been a little confusing. Consider this example:

June constantly worries about her future. To prepare for it, she constantly thinks about it. Specifically, she thinks about how her day will go, what kinds of interactions she will have with her co-workers, and how the dinner with her family will go. Except, instead of thinking about her general, pretty easy-going life, June constantly mentally imagines arguments with her friends, family, and co-workers, to 'better prepare' herself for when those confrontations come.

Now, it is all well and good to prepare yourself for a confrontation when you know—or assume—one is going to happen. If you know that your boss is going to have a serious chat with you, hyping yourself up or going over your past work projects to be prepared is normal and expected. If you believe you are going to have an uncomfortable talk with your parents, mentally going over what they may say and how you will defend yourself, is normal. Notice how each of these things are in the immediate build-up? June's example did not have that build-up. It was her daily mentality.

This type of thinking is exhausting, and it encourages your brain to build negative thought patterns around conflict and other areas of your life. Remember the introduction and that segment about your brain? The more you think about something, the stronger those thoughts and memories will be in your mind, making those brain chemical reactions stronger in your body.

This is all well and good when these are happy or good emotional responses to healthy situations, but when it is about situations which have not come to pass, we are beginning to waste a lot of mental energy on things that do not deserve that much mental output. Additionally, we are not really preparing ourselves for anything. We are not even stopping the worry that we originally wanted to fix.

Reminder

If you connected with any of what was said above,

remember to breathe. It is okay if this happens to you. The first step is awareness, and now you have that.

Take a moment if you need to, and let's keep going.

Painful Rumination

There are always going to be those times when we remember that painfully embarrassing moment in our pre-teen, teen, or young adult years where we consciously made a decision, which in hindsight, was maybe not the best thing to do. However, in non-overthinking brains, these types of instances are very occasional, and are often remembered with a small wince and the ability to move past that particular occasion.

Overthinkers, on the other hand, painfully rethink and relive multiple moments in their lives, which honestly may not even be worthy of that much memory. However, by that point, their brain has made this type of thinking a habit, and they may not even be consciously aware of what they are doing. On top of that, they painfully ruminate, which means they re-think their thoughts repetitively over every single aspect of the situation using emotions like regret, self-loathing, and self-blame (Welle (www.dw.com), 2020).

Overthinkers constantly do this. They constantly remind themselves of painful memories and continue to overanalyze scenarios which are no longer in their control, and have no possibility to be solved. Now, there is a clear line between looking at a recent scenario in hindsight and admitting where you could have done better, versus painfully ruminating over something.

For instance, say you recently went through a breakup. Many people will agree there is a reasonable length of time where it is socially acceptable to admit your own fault in the breakup. Saying things like, "Well, that was my mistake," or "In hindsight, I could have done this better," and then using those reflections to better prepare yourself for your next relationship, is in no way painfully ruminating over the breakup. However, if you are reflecting on a breakup with thoughts like, "I should have been more supportive," "I have lost my soulmate," or "I am unlovable," then those thoughts are sadly one hundred percent painful rumination and overthinking behaviors (Welle (www.dw.com), 2020).

The Difference

If you are still unsure, let's examine the two examples more closely. The first instance admits where they had done wrong, but does not make the other person an angel in the relationship. Instead, they clearly defined boundaries around what they did wrong, and what they could change in themselves.

In comparison, the second person does not even focus on bettering themselves at all, but rather on how unattractive physically and emotionally they are now that they no longer have a partner.

A great antidote for it, as perfectly described by a friend is, "Going to the garden to eat worms." Sometimes, overthinkers become so caught up in the negative cycle of their own thoughts that they begin to spiral to the point where they feel unloved, unworthy, and that they may as well go sit in the garden and eat worms, because no one will stop them or even care enough to stop them. This type of thinking is a result of painful rumination, because we, as overthinkers, painfully ruminate over self-deprecating thoughts to the point where we believe them.

Again, if this is you, do not be ashamed. You are worthy of love, affection, and someone wanting the best for you. You are worthy of wanting the best and getting the best. Do not let the painful rumination win, it is a struggling uphill battle, but together we can do it.

Perfectionism

Perfectionism is something many of us unconsciously strive for. We want to be perfect in that hobby, we want to be perfect for our partner, etc. It may not even seem like perfection to you. It could simply be labeled as wanting to be your 'best.' And best is okay, because the word and colloquialism for that saying generally means that your best changes with you. For example, say you begin to take up running. Giving and doing your best in the beginning may be a short distance, or shorter intervals of running at a time. Yet, as you progress in your running journey, so will your ability to go longer in distance and without breaks, making your best grow with your body.

Perfectionism, on the other hand, does not grow with

you. It limits you. At its very core, perfectionism is the need to be or appear perfect, or to believe that perfection is even possible to achieve. When it comes to perfection in relation to overthinking, there are two main problems. The first is that many people believe that there is such a thing as 'healthy perfectionism' to justify this type of behavior. Except, a better way to describe 'healthy perfectionism' is what was just discussed: trying for our best. In comparison between perfectionism and trying your best, the most distinctive difference is that when you try your best you are willing to admit your best may not be perfect, and that you are opening yourself to failure. This type of vulnerability is hard for anyone, but when you pair it with overthinkers the vulnerability which is required when trying your best becomes almost paralyzing, as it is forcing your brain to begin considering how you might fail.

Which brings up the second problem. Opening yourself up to failure—meaning you are letting yourself be vulnerable—is removing the shield perfectionism provides (Good Therapy, 2019). Sounds odd, right? Think about it. As an overthinker, your brain is fighting multiple things at once. You are fighting your own feelings of inadequacy, plus possibly years of training your brain to think negatively about yourself, while also attempting to be vulnerable enough to admit your failures to yourself and potentially others. Which then makes the shield of perfectionism seem much more safe and easy, because you are still putting in the work—or at least, you think you are—to improve yourself without potentially making a fool of yourself at the same time.

The problem is that perfectionism is almost impossible to maintain constantly, and is definitely exhausting to emulate. Additionally, perfectionism brings with itself a whole new set of problems which latch onto overthinking, such as analysis paralysis and information overload.

How does it do that?

Well, first of all, perfectionism, analysis paralysis, and information overload all stem from the constant thought that we are not good enough. We are not good enough at this hobby, we are not getting better quickly enough, etc., and if we have this innate belief that we must be perfect, then we will of course develop a type of paralysis when we know we cannot achieve that perfectionism immediately. Our brains are too busy thinking about how we can get there and how we can make the physical actions of what we are thinking about be the most perfect the first time around. Additionally, our brain becomes overloaded from all of the information we have shoved into it to try and process the scenario, while simultaneously figuring out how we can be perfect at it our first go-round.

Then, let's not forget the paralysis that comes with this type of thinking. Everything that has been described so far sounds pretty overwhelming. Which is exactly what happens. Your brain is so full with every possible scenario, your fears, your desires, and its inability to think in a new way (due to your overthinking patterns and habits) that it begins to get paralyzed and shut down. What this feels like is when you suddenly freeze or cannot make a decision because you just cannot seem to legitimately think of one.

While those are what happens in an overthinking brain, non-overthinking brains do experience events where they also desire to be perfect. A great example is the term 'bridezilla,' If you are unsure what that term means, it is used to describe a woman who is normally quite reasonable but has become an absolute monster in regards to her wedding. Everything has to be just so, and everything has to be perfect. Even though this example is incredibly specific, it points out how there are certain times when perfectionism is not related to overthinking, but is rather a one-off want or desire motivated by something else entirely. It may still not be incredibly healthy, but if your perfectionism is related to a one-off scenario which will not be repeated, or you do not repeat that need for perfectionism for every one-off scenario, then your overthinking most likely does not manifest in the form of perfectionism.

Similarly, everyone experiences brain paralysis at some point in time, and probably multiple times. Adrenaline athletes experience it almost regularly, as their brain cannot catch up to what their bodies are doing, and they have to rely on instinct and ingrained decision making to ensure that their body does what is necessary in that situation. However, overthinkers tend to experience this kind of paralysis almost daily, and not even in adrenaline-infused situations.

Why?

Because their brain is so busy coming up with ways to ensure that the innate desire for perfection is maintained, while also analyzing every possible bit of information given (along with mental scenarios and play-alongs).

Again, these are all signs of being an overthinker, but you do not have to have all of them. You may experience a combination of them, or some of them may only become apparent in relevant situations. The point is, you are an overthinker because you are literally overthinking everything, including whether you are an overthinker or not.

So, in summary, the cycle goes like this: As an overthinker, you latch onto perfectionism because you do not want to be vulnerable to other people in whatever hobby or scenario it is (or perhaps it is everywhere in your life). Then, because you are trying too hard to be perfect, you begin to develop an information overload on how to maintain that perfection during your action, which then brings up analysis paralysis, because your brain is too busy trying to process all of the information and analyze which is your best bet to get the perfection you want.

Obsession

As has been hinted at in other sections, overthinking has a strong correlation to obsession. When we overthink we tend to begin obsessing over our thoughts. This could be where we went wrong, how we can hide our imperfections, how we can stay perfect, etc. No matter what the actual thought is, it is normally a negative one, which honestly is not the best thing to be obsessing over.

Before getting too offended or upset, it is also reasonably associated that by this point the obsessive thoughts are more so a habit or subconscious thought, which is then brought into the conscious, rather than an active decision. Once your brain is accustomed to making certain types of associations, it will begin automatically making those associations whether we want it to or not; including obsessing over whatever has popped into our mind.

The problem is that for overthinkers, this means that their brain begins to get accustomed to wasting lots of mental energy obsessing over thoughts which do not need to be re-examined. While it sounds harsh, it is true. Going over a negative scenario or thought briefly and succinctly to analyze and make better choices is a great way to learn and begin to emulate self-regulating behaviors. However, overthinkers do not do it briefly, succinctly, or with the goal of actually bettering themselves. Oh, you may have that intent and that may be what you are telling yourself when you go over a scenario for the hundredth time. However, start to ask yourself this question: Is going over this scenario really going to help me be better, or am I using this as an excuse to focus on everything negative in my life and about me?

If your answer is 'yes' to that question, do not lose heart, because you are now aware of what you are doing and why. Take a moment and breathe, because at one point, we have all been there. Even non-overthinkers have moments or phases where they have used something guised as healthy behavior to enable unhealthy habits. The thing is, now that you are aware, you can stop it.

In general, obsession is something which can be either good or bad; it depends on the obsession and how it affects your life. Even being obsessed with physical fitness to the point where you ignore the rest of your life and responsibilities is unhealthy. The same can be said for obsessive thoughts. Sometimes being captivated by a type or way of thinking is normal. Yet, overthinkers use obsessive thoughts to constantly think about the negatives in their life and exemplify every other type of thought which has been discussed so far.

Always Questioning

As you have probably guessed, always questioning does help sometimes when it is a positive way to think or be. For instance, like when you are working on a work project, trying to figure out what clients want, or wanting any type of clarification for immediate situations. The problem with overthinkers is that this constant questioning is not just in positive and required areas. They will always question themselves, and those around them, beyond figuring out what is needed in the moment. A great example would be always asking your partner if they truly love you, or questioning why your parents are willing to help you.

Questioning acts of love, or even basic societal niceties, is a sign of overthinking, because you are questioning things that have given no indication that that type of question is necessary. In general, non-overthinkers do not question if these acts of love, service, or social niceties are deserved or question if they have earned them. Overthinkers, on the other hand, often do. That is not okay because it is putting you in a constant stressful situation. Do not worry, though; we will continue to fight this together and give you ways to begin reframing those questions into healthy and positive ways of thinking.

Stop

Now, there is a good chance that if you are an overthinker, you are suddenly overthinking everything you have read so far and are perhaps questioning yourself, your reality, your thoughts, and maybe even your intentions.

If you are doing that, take a moment to breathe.

Remember, this chapter is to help you affirm that you are overthinking and begin to set the groundwork for noticing when and how you overthink.

Self-Doubt

Ah, self-doubt. This type of thinking is pervasive and can be considered the root for many other forms of thinking which have been discussed so far. So what is it? While it is pretty self-explanatory, just in case this is a term which is unfamiliar to you (which is completely okay), self-doubt is, well, doubting yourself. In regards to overthinking, this type of doubting goes so far as to cause you to begin questioning things you know you can do, to the point where you become self-critical and self-destructive.

In some circumstances, such as a new job, new hobby, or new relationship, doubting yourself and your abilities is a natural and normal response. However, in healthy scenarios, your personal growth and problem-solving skills allow you to proactively fight any self-doubts which occur. For instance, say that you are doubting whether you will be able to maintain a new job.

However, you fight through those doubts and over time begin to overcome them, because you are able to identify your problem areas and proactively confront them. In comparison, overthinkers use their self-doubt as a way to begin cycling into their predominant thought patterns where, instead of looking for proactive solutions to prove they can do something, they get overwhelmed and defeated by their self-doubt, to the point where they are unable to see past their own mental cycles.

Yet, when it comes to overthinkers, self-doubt is incredibly pervasive and hard to identify in some cases, as well as fight. This is mainly because self-doubt so easily attaches itself to other forms of overthinking, such as perfectionism and painful rumination. Self-doubt can be viewed as a gateway into the other forms of overthinking, because the feeling of self-doubt can so easily lead to everything else which has been discussed so far. On closer consideration, it makes sense.

Since the very essence of self-doubt is doubting yourself to the point where you freeze and forget how to do something, even if you know you can do it, your brain is then able to introduce other negative thought patterns on top of those doubts. Why? Because your brain is so used to thinking in negative cycles. If your brain is already accustomed to being negative, and it has gotten to the point where it—and yourself—are disbelieving of being capable of doing anything positive, then it makes sense that the 'next best thing' would be to latch onto negative thought patterns.

Compared to the other forms of overthinking, self-doubt is probably one of the strongest forms used by overthinkers, because it is often used as a reason to not continue on bettering yourself, for the reasons mentioned above.

Post-Read Breathe

This chapter and previous segments were a lot to take in. So now it is time to take a breath. If you have begun to notice some ways that you think align with this section, that is okay. Identifying where you are overthinking and wasting mental energy does not mean you are a failure, it does not mean something is wrong with you, and it does not mean that you are incapable of fixing this if you want to. Awareness is the first step, and this chapter was written with the intent of causing you to raise awareness within and about yourself.

What it does mean is that you will have to start building strong forms of mental self-awareness, which we will discuss in a later chapter.

Now, for the small number of you who may be reading this to try and gain understanding for a loved one who is an overthinker, or to see if this book would be helpful for an overthinker, do not let this chapter get to you. As has been said numerous times, there are plenty of situations where each of these signs are healthy reactions in occasional instances. The key word here is 'occasional.' It is perfectly normal to feel self-doubt when starting a new job in a completely new career. It is one hundred percent okay to be in pain over an old awkward memory from when you were a pre-teen. Those types of thoughts—if they are few and far between—happen to us all, whether we are overthinkers or not.

However, if it is happening frequently, and more than

you would like to admit. It is time to do some deep hard-truth diving into yourself.

Journaling

So, with all of this information in mind, it is time to begin journaling some thoughts, questions, and answers. For these journaling sections, please, be honest with yourself. No one has to see this journal. No one has to know. But it is best to be honest on paper because then at least somewhere on this Earth, you have made the conscious decision to be truthful to yourself.

Take a moment and if you have to re-read parts of this chapter, make sure you do that. But for now, start to think about how you personally overthink. Is there one way in particular that you use, or is it a combination of all of them? Is there a particular trigger that you are aware of for these thoughts, or perhaps for even certain types of these thoughts?

A few great questions to get the ball rolling, and to start

your introspective journey, is to ask yourself the following questions:

- Do you overthink?

- Do you think about thinking?

- Do you catch yourself obsessing over past thoughts or interactions with other people and obsessing about it to the point where you now have raised anxiety?

Chapter 2

The Obsessions and Anxieties
of an Overthinker

Even though the last chapter specifically discussed obsession and anxiety in relation to overthinking, those examples and discussions tended to either give one specific example, or were written with the intent of giving you a good base of understanding for how obsession and anxiety worked with overthinking.

In this chapter, we are going to go into specific types of obsessions and anxieties, specifically in regards to how it is affecting your life through four main areas: habits, relationships, your job, and physical activity and miscellaneous circumstances. To give you as best of an understanding on how obsession and anxiety works with overthinking, this chapter will be divided into three sections. The first two sections will discuss obsessions and anxieties in relation to an overthinking as well as non-overthinking brain, to help you begin to notice when thoughts are related to overthinking, versus a naturally-triggered response to certain situations you might find yourself in. The third section will discuss how obsession and anxieties in relation to overthinking—as well as overthinking in and of itself—may be present within your own life. This section will also include examples and a step-by-step guide to show where the overthinking begins.

Please note, these examples are simply examples. They are meant to be used as a guide for you to begin your journey to awareness and to begin monitoring and noticing certain thought patterns which may be occurring in your own brain.

So, without further ado, let's begin.

Obsessions

According to Merriam-Webster, an obsession is "a persistent disturbing preoccupation with an often unreasonable idea or feeling," or, "broadly: compelling motivation" (Merriam-Webster, n.d.-a). Before diving into the overthinkers and how they tend to obsess, it should first be noted that there is a term going around colloquially called 'healthy obsession.' Essentially, this definition is based on the broad definition of obsession, and is used to bring a new twist on how to implement healthy habits into your life. People who use obsession in a healthy way essentially use the terminology to begin motivating themselves to engage in more healthy habits.

However, when it comes to overthinking, obsession tends to present itself in a more negative light; predominantly through two 'different' ways. (For the purposes of this book, we are going to say two ways, but they are closely interlinked and could arguably be seen as extensions of each other.)

The first way is a form of avoidance, or a way to 'heal' past traumas. Oddly enough, obsession becomes almost like a mental Band-Aid for a past problem which overthinkers cannot resolve, for whatever reason. These reasons could be past traumas, the inability or lack of desire to dig deeper, or perhaps even the inability to continue on their healing journey due to a mental roadblock, confusion on where to go, or the sad fact of being in the middle of doing the grunt work for fixing their mental pathways and how they think. Regardless as to why it has happened, to some overthinkers, obsessing over certain scenarios, relationships, or even the potential 'what ifs' in our lives becomes the magic elixir which will fix all their problems. Which in itself is problematic, because they are not using their obsessive thoughts in a positive way to actually bring about healing and change. This then brings up the second way that obsession can be used by overthinkers: as a form of continuing the worry or negativity cycle.

Let's be honest. We have all been there. We have all experienced days, weeks, perhaps even months or years where everything is constantly going wrong and we see no end in sight to the misery. Maintaining a positive, or even pragmatic, mindset during those times is understandably difficult . Now, take those types of thoughts and feelings of it never getting better, and you begin to get a tiny glimpse into an overthinker's head when it comes to using obsessive thoughts to continue their personal worry or negativity cycle. As mentioned in the previous chapter, these types of thought patterns tend to cause overthinkers to want to go to the garden to eat worms, or causes them to begin to believe the negativity they are thinking about themselves.

These thoughts tend to center around their believed inadequacies and inabilities in every and all situations, relationships, and scenarios. For instance, these types of thoughts tend to present themselves like, "I will never get better," "this situation will never improve," or "I am not capable." Now, none of these thoughts tend to be completely intentional, although self-sabotage can be associated with overthinking. However, in the early stages, most overthinkers actually use obsession as a way to try and problem solve and attempt to stop their worrying about things they cannot control (Relf, 2020).

What makes obsessive thoughts even more pervasive is that they have this awful ability to affix themselves to actual aspects of your life, making your personal awareness of where and how you overthink (if at all) that much harder to decipher. As seen in the above examples, obsessive thoughts caused by overthinking have no rhyme or reason to them; they simply latch onto whatever they are able to.

We will discuss how those manifest in different areas of your life, but first, let's finish up the preliminary discussions by talking about anxiety.

Anxiety

The Merriam-Webster dictionary defines 'anxiety' as an: " apprehensive uneasiness or nervousness usually over an impending or anticipated ill: a state of being anxious" (Merriam-Webster, 2019). Anxiety has become a bit of a buzz-word lately, and that is not to diminish anyone's personal journey with anxiety, or even to belittle the actual necessity for understanding and recognizing anxiety and its multiple forms and manifestations within different people and their lives.

Actually, that statement is meant to be one of joy. No

longer can people say that you are simply "overthinking things," or that "it is not that bad," because anxiety is bad. It is bad for you, and what it does to your brain long term. The problem is that unless it is a shared anxiety, such as the global pandemic of 2020, anxiety is not really something which can be shared or understood. Yes, people can use their own experiences with anxiety to help you —the previous statement was not at all suggesting that people cannot help you with anxiety—but what is trying to be explained here is how singular each person's anxiety is.

This makes it all the more applicable and easy for an overthinking mind to attach to. Just like with obsession, anxiety has certain incredibly justifiable manifestations and scenarios, where it is almost more concerning that you are not feeling anxiety, rather than feeling it. For example, a situation like that could be if you were in the middle of a massive physical confrontation. There are very, very few people who could be in a massive mob and not feel some form of anxiety or adrenaline rush, and those types of people are most likely not overthinkers.

So, if there are times where anxiety is a bit more 'normal,' then what does it look like with overthinkers? Well, as with obsession, it is not that it pops up in unnecessary or even unjustifiable moments. It is that anxiety becomes a daily occurrence, and it is the thought and action pattern that your brain continues to thrive on; it has become the first, maybe even only response. Yes, this is also what suffering with anxiety can potentially look like, and sometimes overthinking does lead to problems with obsession, anxiety, and depression. Which is why obsession and anxiety are being more thoroughly discussed in this chapter.

Understanding that anxiety and obsession are strong emotional thoughts which are uniquely singular to you and how your brain functions with those emotions, plus the overthinking stimuli of your brain, is what makes you unique. It is also the main thing you need to begin analyzing and understanding about yourself. Having these thoughts more than 'normal' people is not a bad thing. Overthinking and being an anxious person does not make you less of a functioning adult. It simply means that your brain is not being kind to you, and you are going to have to put work into fixing that in order to have a better life in the long term.

Your brain is stuck. It is as simple as that. How you got to being stuck is irrelevant in this immediate moment (it will be important later). Right now, all you need to do is recognize that unfortunately, due to these anxious and obsessive thoughts, your overthinking brain has allowed itself to program these thoughts into literally everything, or that one particular part, of your life, and it is going to be hard to train it to let go.

How It Affects Your Life

This brings us to how overthinking, anxiety, and obsessive thoughts affect your life. Chances are, they have been affecting your life more than you know or are willing to admit to yourself. Now is not the time to continue in denial, even if it is just to yourself and the journal for this section, be honest. Really look at your life, your brain, your habits, your fears, and your triggers. Begin to look at the examples and see if anything manifests with you; no similarity is too small.

The whole point of this segment is to look and see where your overthinking has latched onto, and how it is causing you to behave.

The Habit

Habits may seem like an odd thing to mention, since we are discussing how overthinking manifests itself into your life, but that's just it. It is a habit. Remember the introduction? By obsessively thinking and allowing those thoughts to come in, your brain was building strong negative neural pathways which caused this type of thinking to become a habit. A very bad one.

Regardless of whether you intentionally built this habit or not (it would surprise many of you to know how often negative habits are built through unintentional actions), sadly, overthinking is a habit (Koa Foundations, n.d.). And it has manifested itself into your daily routine, however that looks.

The good news is that all habits can be changed, including negative mental ones. The bad news is that this will not be instantaneous, because it is going to require a lot of mental work to ensure that you make a good foundation on how to recognize your overthinking and what to do with it.

Relationships

Ah, relationships. The breeding ground of overthinking, anxieties, and obsessive thoughts for anyone, let alone someone who specifically deals with an overthinking brain. For this section, remember that what will be discussed here will be mainly for any type of relationship which is non-professional. This includes: family, friends, children, spouses, significant others, extended family, and even your peers and acquaintances (like the people at the gym or coffee shop).

So, the first question is, why is it so easy for overthinking, obsessive, and anxious thoughts to show up here? Because they involve other people. It sounds strange, but it is true. When you are combating an overthinking brain, an anxious brain, an obsessive brain, or a winning combination of all three, it is highly possible that another person is actually low-key stressing you out. This stress has absolutely nothing to do with the person, or even the relationship, necessarily. It more so has to do with the fact that unless your relationship is bordering on the over-communicative, there is a very good chance that sooner or later, you are going to begin questioning certain things in that relationship.

All it takes is that one wrong word, that one mis-step, or that one odd action in a daily occurrence to cause an overthinker's brain to begin going off like a firework display. Which, when you think about it, makes sense. By the very definition of an overthinker, they overthink something to the point where it becomes unhealthy (hence the obsession or anxiety). For example, let's say that you are an overthinker and the following happens:

Your friend Allen, whom you text faithfully every day (and normally throughout the day) about your troubles and anything and everything, does not text you back all morning. Not concerned, you send a text asking if they are okay and then go about your own work. However, there is still no reply at lunch. You are now beginning to feel anxious, and you start to wrack your brain to see if you can remember him mentioning anything about not being available for the day. Nothing comes to mind. By mid-afternoon, you are now an anxious mess, scrolling through your past text messages to see if there is some hidden clue in a well-placed emoji, comma, sentence, or word choice, to see if you had somehow annoyed them and had missed it. When that does not work, you begin to obsessively think and tear apart all of your previous conversations to see what went wrong. By the end of the day, you are convinced that they are no longer your friend and that the relationship is doomed, waiting for the strike of a masterful keystroke to end a friendship. You are devastated. However, by evening, Allen texts you back saying that he had forgotten his phone at home, and had to stay late at work in meetings and asks about your day. Completely forgetting the entire day you just spent filled with anxiety and negative thoughts, you answer Allen, and suddenly everything is alright with the world.

Does this type of scenario sound familiar to you? All it took was one change in a normal daily occurrence and then a lack of response to your inquiries to trigger a downward spiral of obsessive, anxious, and overthinking thoughts.

Now, before showing where things went wrong, let's go

through some positives first. Take note of these positives, add them to your journal at the end of this segment, and meditate on how you can use these in a future chapter. The first positive is that you noticed your friend had not texted you and instead of immediately thinking you did something, you asked if they were okay.

It is hard with an overthinking, obsessive, and anxious brain, but sometimes when a regular relationship is different, it has absolutely nothing to do with you. They could be having a bad day or have a rushed morning. Asking and clarifying with them first is a great way to show you care and stave off overthinking tendencies.

The second positive is that you were able to not overthink the question. This step will take a while to get to, but once you get there, it is a really nice place to be. What is this step? It is simple. This step was how you asked Allen if he was okay, then went back to work. Some might find this a little stand-offish, and perhaps even rude, but going back to work and not allowing yourself to worry until lunch time (in the example) is a great exercise for an overthinker's brain, because it is allowing the other person to respond to your question without you beginning to create a narrative in your head, or come up with situations that would cause a negative mental cycle, which would cause your day to go downhill.

The third positive was how you went back through your text history and memory to see if Allen had mentioned not being available, and you had temporarily forgotten. Misremembering or forgetting that type of information is totally natural; we all do it sometimes, and then we are able to laugh it off when we remember and go about our day. Making this the third step before overthinking and worrying is another great way to begin gaining perspective and maintaining a slight bit of sanity before the overthinking takes hold.

Okay, so with those positives out of the way, it is time to start looking at the overthinking, obsession and anxiety thoughts, all of which were pretty obvious to see. Notice in the example how the longer Allen kept quiet, the worse the negative mental cycles became? You started to tear apart the texts looking for hidden clues, and then by the end of the day, you had convinced yourself that you had somehow upset Allen to the point where he would not even tell you what was wrong, and were already in the mourning period for that relationship.

Talk about a mental and emotional roller coaster. Now, again, this is not your fault in the sense that while you willingly chose to think that way, we are going to assume that you have had years (and maybe some actual experiences) to prove that this kind of thinking is accurate. Yes, you made the conscious choice to begin mourning the relationship with Allen, but not only did you stave off your overthinking for a short period of time, you most likely were even unaware of the mental thoughts which caused you to begin obsessing over every line of text and emojis.

But are you not tired of thinking this way? As someone who fights overthinking daily, it is exhausting just remembering the constant mental circles and emotional rides the brain can take you on if you are not in control of it. But do not be fooled, it takes a long time to get there, and the journey will involve looking into yourself and how that type of thinking got in.

Job

Overthinking is often something which pops up in the workforce, and that could be for a variety of valid reasons, such as a lack of communication between managers, staff, and business requirements, or perhaps it is because there was a conflict which was never fully resolved. Unfortunately, the corporate world has many, many reasons and ways where overthinking becomes an actual form of self-defense. However, since overthinkers tend to use the overthinking mental cycle to bring up negative thoughts and end up believing them, this can take a relatively toxic predisposition for a certain environment, and make it hundreds of times worse.

Compared to other manifestations of overthinking, it can become pretty obvious when you are overthinking in your job, because it will have a direct correlation to your performance. For instance, you can longer handle deadlines, you need to be overinformed on projects to the point where you are micromanaging other people, you cannot sleep, and you have problems making decisions, even when you used to make those decisions with barely any effort (Malin, 2021).

While to many people these symptoms could appear to be burnout (overthinking and burnout can be related and happen at the same time), there are finite differences. Essentially, burnout results in a lack of incentive, whereas overthinking causes you to freeze and be unable to finish. Both scenarios result in you fighting to complete a work-related project, but the reasonings behind completing the action are different. Consider the following examples:

James cannot handle deadlines at his job. He will know about a deadline months in advance, but continue to push off completing the project until the very last minute, because that is the only way he is able to think clearly and succinctly about what has to be done, and how.

For every project that he works on, Avery needs absolutely every possible piece of information, including the things that he does not need to know in order to complete his share of the work. If any task or project requires him to do input without having every possible scenario covered, Avery is unable to do the project without multiple team member's input and help.

Alison is normally a very good decision maker at work, and as a manager, she should be. However, something has changed. Every time a decision has to be made, Alison freezes and becomes unable to see the clear outcomes of each choice, and has developed a sense of 'buyers remorse' when she actually does make a decision at work. Even if it is the right decision, she will doubt that it was the right one for the project or her team.

Each person mentioned in the examples above exhibits how their overthinking has hindered something which is a requirement for their job, and in some cases, was something that they had not previously struggled with. James, for instance, cannot work on a project until it is right to the deadline, which has become a coping mechanism to combat the overthinking he experiences while working on the project. Avery is unable to get out of his head enough to be able to handle spontaneous projects, meaning his overthinking brain has developed perfectionism and analysis paralysis. Alison has developed overthinking to the point where she now doubts her decisions, which used to not occur.

When reading it on paper, it is pretty obvious in each instance where overthinking has hindered someone's ability to work, but it can be pretty hard to spot when the overthinking is within your own brain, or the overthinker is someone you know very well. The key with workplace overthinking is to gain perspective and hindsight on when to notice if you are overworked, overstressed, or overthinking, and that is something that comes with self-awareness and hindsight.

Physical and Extracurricular Activity

Many people understand and agree that overthinking takes over every part of their lives, yet physical activity or extracurricular activities is not often thought of when making that statement. Part of it is because it takes so much longer to begin noticing how overthinking hurts those parts of our lives.

For instance, with physical activity, overthinking may not come in until much later, because being active gives your brain a rush of endorphins, or 'happy hormones,' which allow your brain to stave off any type of negative spiral downwards. When overthinking does finally cross the threshold into our physical activities, it is so easily guised as a 'bad day,' a 'sign we need to take more rest days,' or 'leveling up.' Think about it. In any of those above scenarios, our brains are constantly fighting any type of negative thought combined with the ever-so optimistic 'if only' scenario to create the juxtaposition that we have to change something in order to be better. For many of us, we do make that change, and we do become better. But what about those times when we do not become better? What about when we let those defeatist thoughts win, or cause us to change how we approach the activity?

That right there, is how overthinking can hurt your physical activity. It is all well and good to think about your limits and begin to realistically contemplate if the next step of your physical journey is one you want to take, but when we let those thoughts become more negative than normal, the spiral begins.

Consider this example:

You have been doing this physical activity for a few

years now, and you know that you have been improving, but then you hit a natural plateau. Unphased for a while, you push through, take more rest days, and begin to prepare for when your body is able to hurtle to the next level. but that leveling up is taking longer than you thought. Over the next few weeks, your thoughts are less optimistic and more pessimistic, you begin to start failing at things you had no problem completing before, and your previous "I can do it" thoughts become more negative and self-loathing, such as "Wow, now I cannot even do this, I am doing great" (infuse lots of anger and sarcasm into that statement).

Notice how in this example everything started out great. You were preparing for the level up, you were doing everything right, but when it took longer than you thought, that was when you let your guard down and allowed overthinking and a negative downward spiral to get to you. Do not worry; it is highly acknowledged that it is all fine and dandy to sit here typing that statement out, but you are the one actually feeling it. Well, believe it or not, that feeling has been felt in physical activities before. Many times. Combating and fighting the overthinking aspect, while also dealing with physical inadequacies or extra training to meet certain goals, is not fun. Which is where accountability partners or safe people come into play. Doing physical activity with upbeat people will help combat your overthinking and help you begin to implement practices which will be discussed in a future chapter.

And with that, onto the extracurricular activities, or, for the context of this book, social activities. When it comes to social circles, clubs, or activities where being social is the main objective, it is pretty easy for overthinking to sneak in there. The problem is that compared to a relationship, overthinking presents itself differently in how we handle it. For most people, overthinking in regards to a club or some type of social extracurricular activity results in no longer participating, or being delayed or avoidant of that situation. This happens because the negative downward spiral has caused you to begin believing all of the awful things your brain has been telling you.

For instance: Laura has been part of her boating club for years. She enjoys the activity and the people, and normally has a great time. She is even on the committee and helps out with fundraisers and maintaining the boats in the off season. However, due to circumstances which were out of her control, some of the last few fundraisers did not bring in as much money as they would normally, and Laura had begun to feel self-conscious about it. This caused her overthinking to begin working its way into how she thought about the club and her role in it. Over the next few weeks, members and friends noticed that Laura was not as chipper, and had begun to not be at the club as often. She had also begun to skip meetings and was not as attentive or involved in planning events like before.

Again, notice how all it took was one negative thing and Laura's brain was able to easily push overthinking into that area of her life. In this instance, Laura's overthinking caused her to withdraw, most likely due to thoughts of her not being good enough and feeling like someone else would do a better job at those events than her. The more her thoughts spiraled, the more she withdrew.

In each example, overthinking was not immediately present; and this is something that you really need to notice and pay attention to. Just because you are an overthinker does not necessarily mean it will take over every area of your life immediately. It definitely has the ability to, and for some people it sadly will, but for the lucky few, there may be a few areas of their lives that are insulated from that type of thinking. Normally, that is because those areas of life have little room for negativity, either because there are too many happy emotions and thought processes related to it already, or the opportunity has not arisen.

This is important: You cannot be lazy in watching how you think in those areas. As you saw in the examples—and as you have learned—overthinking can creep into anything if you give it space to. Including areas of your life which are currently just fine.

Thankfully, once you have become comfortable fighting your overthinking, it will become a habit, and you will not have to pay special attention to these areas of your life.

Journal

Well, this chapter was a lot to take in. Now we come to the good stuff. It is time for you to make a cup of tea or coffee and begin to really think about everything you have read in this chapter.

Did you notice any similarities in the examples? If so, what were they? Let your thoughts and mind wander down that trail for a bit. You could be surprised by what comes up.

Next up, remember those positive attributes that were in some examples? Pull them up and begin to look at them again. Notice how these positive actions are small and easy to add as a step to stop your overthinking brain from immediately jumping into crisis mode. Write down the ones that really resonate with you, and begin to come up with mantras, or ways to remind yourself to use them before overthinking.

Finally, look at the areas of your life (if any) where you do not overthink. Make a special point of keeping these areas of your life in the front of your brain in the coming chapters.

CHAPTER 3

Eliminate Through Awareness

It may seem a bit like an oxymoron, since part of overthinking is that you are hyper-aware of your brain and yourself, but there is a common trend which has been peeking up and throughout all of the previous parts of this book so far. Your hyper-aware, overthinking brain is only aware of the negatives around you. From the negatives about the situation, to hyper-focusing on all of the negatives about you personally, there have probably been very few moments where your brain has allowed you to be positive and actually find a usable solution.

It is in those moments where awareness comes in. Being aware is so much more than noticing when you are on a negative cycle, or that you are beginning to overthink; even though that is a good place to start. However, to truly begin combatting your overthinking brain, you need to be aware of everything around it. You need to be aware of what you are overthinking about, why you are overthinking about it, and how your brain has decided to overthink to 'solve' the problem or circumstance that is facing.

It takes time to get to this stage. It could take you weeks, months, maybe even years. But the hard work and consistency that you put into figuring out and building up your awareness consistently—even through your overthinking phases—will pay off. Just like with so many other things in our lives, what you put into this section of your overthinking journey, will directly correlate into what comes out of it.

Why You Need It

Some of you may be wondering why you even need self-awareness. Being self-aware of your overthinking may seem like enough, but in reality, it is not. Many overthinkers are aware that they overthink; they may even be aware of when they are actually overthinking. The problem is that when your brain is overthinking, it has the ability to turn into a runaway train. Everyone knows what is happening, but no one is able to stop it. Your brain has become that powerful because you consciously, or unconsciously, continue to dwell on those negative thoughts and related thought patterns. However, do not worry. Your brain is able to bounce back; it will just require more effort and awareness on your part to tear down those habits and put new ones in place. The good news is that once you have created new mental pathways and habits, it will become easier to stick to those than to return to overthinking over time.

Awareness and Overthinking

Normally, awareness is used as an overall term to describe your ability to understand and know yourself. Being aware is how our brains naturally begin to grow, change, and adapt to circumstances that are new, or need us to change in order to do something. That is, in fact, exactly how awareness will be used in this book; just on a deeper level. To truly combat overthinking with awareness, you need to be able to understand when and why you are overthinking. You need to be able to understand and differentiate between when you are going into negativity, worrying, fixating, ruminating, obsessing, or your anxiety cycles while you are overthinking. You need to understand what triggered it, and most of all, you will need the awareness and ability to go back to that scenario or situation later on and gain hindsight on what triggered the overthinking.

Understanding how you personally begin to overthink brings up a new step of self-awareness, because it will help you catch yourself as your overthinking begins to take over. Similarly, you need to begin implementing habits to stop your overthinking, or to go back to those episodes where you can apply hindsight. Figuring out why certain things triggered you will be crucial in your ability to stop overthinking and to begin rewiring your brain to not overthink in the face of those triggers.

Gaining that next level of awareness in regards to your

overthinking is going to be a journey. It will not be easy to see how fragile certain parts of your emotions or mind are, or have gotten over time, but embracing that vulnerability through awareness and deciding to strengthen it through change and habit in fighting overthinking will help you turn the corner mentally.

Implementing Awareness

When it comes to implementing awareness, you have to understand that it will start as a chore which will eventually become a habit. Just like how overthinking is a habit, everything you are going to do to combat it, will also overtime become a habit. The replacement habit, if you will.

The other problem with implementing awareness is that in order to use it to stop your overthinking, you have to actually start becoming present in your everyday life. The good news is that this is now something everyone deals with, thanks to the rise of technology, social media, the news, and constant distractions from our smart devices and how often they are in our hands, or on our person. With so many distractions, it is pretty easy to not stay present in every single moment of the day, which is actually quite sad, when you think about it. Or, so many of us are so busy with our lives that we are constantly thinking one to three steps ahead. Our days become a list, and we tell ourselves we will enjoy life when we are done, but we are never done. No matter which of these scenarios it is, overthinking brains have it hundreds of times worse, because they are either so busy fixating on something else or shutting down from being overwhelmed that being in the present is like looking directly into a stage spotlight. It is blinding, it is painful, and it (the brain) does not want to do it.

Understandable. The present is most likely where overthinking is being triggered and therefore something painful, unresolved, or activating has happened; and although being present in that scenario is never fun, you have to start doing it. Your awareness will not develop and persist in tougher situations if you do not begin to build that habit now.

Finding the time and ways to be present is tricky, but

definitely worth the effort. Introducing ways to be present really depends on where you notice that you disassociate the most, but here are a few quick tips to get you started. First, you can begin to practice being more present by taking several deep and intentional breaths. Pay attention to your body and your surroundings as you breathe, and come back to the present rather than hiding in your brain. Second, you can pay more attention to your surroundings by stopping any type of multitasking. Part of the reason we are not always present is because our brains are already so busy making sure we finish everything we said we would do, while not dying (like texting and crossing the street), that being present is absolutely not an option. Third, you can accept things as they are. That is it. Just accept. Do not try to change, do not try to adapt, do not even necessarily react. Just be there and accept it.

Before going any further, we need to iron something out. This chapter and section is the build up for the next chapter (as it is with all books); however, here we are going to specifically discuss how to implement the habit of awareness in your life. This habit of awareness is going to then be subsumed into the next chapter, meaning that the next chapter is written with the understanding that you have begun the steps listed below, to start building and implementing your self-awareness.

How to Build a Habit

So, before discussing ways to begin implementing awareness into your mental patterns, we are going to briefly discuss how to even successfully implement a habit. Some of you may be incredibly familiar with this concept, and if that is so, feel free to skip this section. But just in case this is something many of you have not consciously done in a while, here are a few things to know and do to be successful.

First is understanding how long it takes. It takes roughly 21 days to make a habit, and about 90 days to make it into a pattern or unconscious decision. If you have done anything in the world of physical fitness, this pattern and concept will not be new to you. However, with those specific 'deadlines' in place, open up a calendar and begin mapping out how long some of these things might take for you if you started today, next week, or even next month. Visually seeing how long it will take you might seem a bit disheartening, but do not let that get to you. Everyone has the same timeline, and no one is exempt from that length of time in creating or maintaining a new habit and fostering it into a lifestyle. You are not alone, and you can do this. But you need to be aware of the long-haul you are in for.

Alright, now onto the nitty gritty stuff.

Start Small

Picking a small thing to do consistently that will not add to your stress, or become an hour-long new blocked out time in your calendar, is one of the ways you can ensure that your habits actually stick. When it comes to awareness, this could be something like implementing a five-minute daily check-in with yourself on your commute home, after dinner, or before bed. If you decide to use this example, make sure that you set a timer. This will ensure you are not creating a scheduled overthink time of your day, while allowing your overthinking brain time to adjust itself and bringing in self-awareness in your day. It is amazing what even allowing five minutes of non-fixation thinking can do for your brain to help it feel refreshed and actually more willing to be mindful throughout the upcoming days.

Small Note

Now, if there are moments, days, or times when these five minutes become negative, that is okay. Sometimes we need to be negative to get the negativity out. But be sure to use your practice at awareness to acknowledge your feelings without letting them spiral out of control.

Practice Daily

If you ever practiced an instrument, or trained for specific fitness goals, you know there are unlimited benefits to practicing something daily, even if it is for brief periods of time. Low-key, daily practice (especially when you are just starting out) will help your body and mind tolerance and discipline grow with you. Using the example of the five-minute awareness check-in, if you practice it daily, you may be able to up that time to 10 minutes after a few weeks, and so on and so forth. When it comes to awareness, daily practice will also help clear your brain and give you the ability to begin upping the awareness to become a constant, subconscious frame of mind (which is what we want), to help you combat overthinking before it even starts.

Stack Your Habits

This may sound a bit odd, but stacking a habit is putting a new habit onto an old habit or routine, to help ensure it actually sticks with you for longer than the original 21 days. Thankfully, there are many apps which can help you build this kind of routine and begin to stack habits on top of each other. Continuing with the example of practicing five-minute awareness check-ins daily, you could stack that habit onto any pre-existing habit like your commute to and from work, your post-work workout, or your nighttime routine to wind down from your day.

No matter how you go about introducing awareness into your life, remember, it is a habit. Specifically, it is going to be the habit to replace overthinking (along with a few others which will be mentioned later). Remember: Nature hates a vacuum, so if you do not have something to replace your overthinking with, you are going to end up right back where you started.

Stop!

Which brings us to the first way to implement awareness. Quite simply: stop. Stop overthinking.

This does not mean stop overthinking in general, because that would be pretty hard (and uncomfortable) to do immediately if you do not have a backup way of thinking. What is meant is to take the reins of when you are overthinking and consciously stop your brain when it begins to go down a negative spiral. This is where your newfound awareness habit comes into play. Being aware of when you are overthinking will allow you to stop. You may not stop immediately, and you may not stop for the entire day, but beginning to notice your thoughts and stop them will go a long way in future steps.

Also, remember: You may slip a few times and you may not catch your overthinking every single time in the beginning. That is okay. This practice is something which will grow with you the longer you do it. So do not give up, and keep going.

Slow Down

Immediately after stopping your thoughts, slow them down. Part of the reason our brains are able to get away with overthinking is because it is a whirlwind. One minute we are simply worrying about an incredibly valid thing, and then next thing we know, we are suddenly on this runaway brain train on thoughts and negative cycles we were not even aware were a problem (sometimes).

Forcing your brain to slow down will allow you to notice where your overthinking brain is going, and to continue consciously stopping those thoughts. this step is incredibly hard and takes a lot of focus, energy, and practice. How to slow down your thoughts is easier said than done. It is to simply begin to almost snail-like process each individual thought and emotion that is going through your brain. Implementing it really depends on what works for you. Some people prefer to get into an almost meditative state through closed eyes and deep breathing, some prefer to go to a quiet space, or to put in earphones. For other people, it is achieved through sheer determination and willpower. Finding the method that works for you will be a trial and error type of method, but once you find it, you have struck gold.

Take Control of Your Emotions

Slowing down your thoughts will then allow you to implement the next step of self-awareness: controlling your emotions. Our emotions are hard to control because so many of them are instantaneous reactions to something happening around us. They sometimes happen without us even fully recognizing that that is what we have done.

A great way to stop this type of emotional reaction is to stop and slow down your brain. Slowing your brain and its thoughts will allow you the space to begin evaluating what emotion you are using and reacting with, and even give you the ability to recognize and decide if that is the right or appropriate emotion for the scenario.

Honestly, this will not happen all of the time. Even people with gold-level awareness will still cry or scream when frightened or in an incredibly high-risk situation. Being calm in those moments takes years of training, and is something that you not only have to work up to, but something you would repeatedly have to put yourself into to create and maintain. Which is not what this book is discussing. In this step, we are discussing the ability to not immediately lash out, either verbally or in our minds, when someone slights us, or to be able to notice and dissect our emotions when we notice we are overthinking and continuing a worry or maintain a negative cycle in our minds.

Before some of you begin to think that controlling your emotions means to stop them, that is absolutely not what is being said here. Controlling your emotions is simply being able to decide what emotion you are going to think with and which one you are going to act on. Being hurt or upset when there is an actual slight or wrong against you is completely valid and something you should never be ashamed of. It is how you react to it and display those emotions where things can get a bit messy. Whether you know it or not, overthinking in response to a trigger is actually a display of those emotions, even if you are the only one to witness the overthinking. At the end of the day, overthinking is a reaction to someone's action or a situation; and you can have complete control over those. Being upset is valid. Being angry is valid. Overthinking those scenarios to the point where your anxiety, depression, or any other type of negative thinking—while valid because you are still feeling them—is maybe not the healthiest way for you to process those emotions.

Journal

Now that you are armed with ways to build your self-awareness, it is time to begin deep diving into yourself. Ask yourself these questions and think about them for a while. Let your brain and emotions begin to really look into the answers.

- How self-aware are you right now?

- How can you implement self-awareness daily?

- Is there a pre-existing habit you can stack it onto?

- How are you going to remind yourself to stop when you notice that you are starting to overthink?

- How are you going to begin slowing down your thoughts to control your emotions?

- Are you willing to begin learning to try and control your emotions?

- Do you need or have an accountability partner?

CHAPTER 4

The Quickest Way to Stop Overthinking

Stopping something like overthinking has essentially two parts to it. The first, which is covered in this chapter, discusses actual tactics and things you can begin doing immediately, or within the relative short-term, to begin the journey. The second step, which is covered in the next chapter, deals with more long-term continuations of what is discussed in the first step.

This chapter is going to build on what was discussed in the previous one in regards to self-awareness. Meaning, that these steps are going to assume that you are working on building and strengthening your mental awareness, and will have steps to which will include that type of mindset and practice. Additionally, how you go about building and implementing your self-awareness (i.e. the section on how to implement and build habits) will be incredibly useful for beginning to start the following principles and changes in your current mind patterns.

Cognitive Replacement

Have you ever heard of the saying that nature abhors a vacuum? What it is referring to is the concept that everything in this world, from nature to our inner bodies, has an action and reaction balance, and when that balance is put off-kilter, something adapts to replace what originally goes missing. You can see this in the world with how animals adapt to being around cities (i.e. birds needing new nesting spots, so finding them on condominium balconies or in trees they normally would not use), to how our bodies adapt to not having certain enzymes or abilities. The same is said for your mind. Fixing overthinking is not simply to just stop and go about your day. Your brain will not handle that well, because there is now all of this unused energy, thought patterns, and intention on what your brain was about to do.

Which is where cognitive replacement comes in. Cognitive replacement is essentially replacing a way your brain thinks or behaves. This could be something as simple as rewiring your brain for how it attempts problem solving, to trying to create more intentional focus times by stopping or rerouting daydreams to pre-allocated time periods. In regards to overthinking, cognitive replacement is replacing your overthinking thoughts with something different.

Preferably these replacement thoughts are positive and more helpful to your brain, day, and overall processes than what your overthinking has so far brought to the table. Yes, that sounds harsh, and it was meant to. Your overthinking brain, while there are times it is incredibly justifiable, has not done you any favors in regards to your mental health and how you are able to think. Yes, you can do this. No, becoming an overthinker was not your goal, intention, or really your fault. But at the same time, you have continued it—consciously or unconsciously—and it is time to grab a hold of it and begin to change that pattern. Starting with cognitive replacement.

Building off of the habits section in the last chapter, begin to think of ways that you can proactively begin to put cognitive replacement into your daily routine. This could be like implementing a gratitude practice when your brain begins to start a negative trajectory, or having a scrap of paper beside you to write out what you are frustrated with and how you can actually begin to solve that problem. Cognitive replacement does not have to be this grand, 12-step program. It can be as difficult or as easy as you want it to be.

Since we are starting off easy and with the little things; it is really recommended that you choose the easy route.

Self-Awareness and Hindsight

As mentioned in the previous chapter, self-awareness is one of the key ingredients in fighting overthinking and stopping those brain patterns. Including hindsight into your self-awareness tactics will be a great way to step up your awareness progress as well as to begin to retrain your mind to find new forms of awareness to begin implementing.

In case this is a term that is new to you, hindsight refers to looking back at a scenario, conversation, or even an emotion, to figure out the cause, why and how you felt and reacted that way, and if that reaction was what you wanted to exhibit; and if not, how you can change that for next time.

Hindsight is a great learning tool to help overcome overthinking because it forces you to break down scenarios into piece-by-piece mini-bites of compacted information. You take one action and bundle it with your thoughts and feelings about that action, then begin to analyze how and why it worked or not. This also provides you with a great self-learning technique which can be used in future instances.

For example: Josh was having a frustrating day at work. Everything that could go wrong was going wrong.

During his lunch break, Josh took a moment to look back at some of the scenarios he had just gone through, to see how he had handled them. While analyzing, he noted that most of the interactions and reactions were handled well on his end, and only one was a bit negative and had caused him to begin spiraling slightly. Even though he had caught the beginnings of his overthinking spiral, Josh took a look at that incident more closely.

It was about a special work project with a few of his team members. The project was not going well and one of the team members was blatantly ignoring Josh's role in the group, which was to edit the other person's work. This had been going on for awhile, but today, on top of everything else, the person's attempts at justifying their inability to do what Josh needed them to do were just too much. While he did not yell at them, Josh was definitely short and a little more curt than he normally was. After the team member had left, Josh had then unintentionally spent 10 minutes mentally fuming at his co-worker and getting nothing done. In the present, Josh was analyzing why he had been so short-tempered with his coworker and that entire interaction. He mentally acknowledged his frustrations and made a note in his day timer to talk with their manager about how team roles could be changed, or needed to be enforced, and then began to look at his emotions and reactions. Josh studied what had made him so frustrated, what he was responsible for in that frustration, and what he could do to begin minimizing those frustrations and his actions in the future. Additionally, he began to identify certain triggers, and walked through scenarios on how he could avoid being that short-tempered in the future (if at all possible). He also went and apologized to his co-worker after lunch.

This was a bit of a long example, so let's break it down. We will start off with the positives first. In this example, Josh immediately recognized that he needed to re-analyze and evaluate the scenario with his coworker. This is a good thing, because it shows Josh's self-awareness and his recognition that hindsight (or being more removed from that scenario) would help him be able to figure out responsibilities and give a fresh outlook on things. Josh also recognized and validated his frustrations. Nowhere in this book can it be said that your emotions are invalid. However, Josh recognized that while his emotions were valid, his reaction and response to them, were not. Additionally, Josh took his frustrations and made a proactive action out of them by making a note to discuss this coworker with a manager, to try and resolve the issue. Next, Josh then began to parse over the interaction to decide what was his responsibility (also known as boundary), and which of those responsibilities he could fix or help with, compared to what he was not responsible for. Josh then began to make plans for how to avoid and fix his boundaries or frustrations in the future, and then ended that entire thought session by apologizing to his coworker.

Small Note

Some of you may think that the apology to the coworker was unnecessary, and that is a case-by-case and personal decision. In this instance, it was necessary, because the coworker received more frustration from Josh than was appropriate for the situation.

As you can see through this example, hindsight is an excellent tool to combat overthinking. An overthinking brain with no control or good habits would have taken that scenario and made it worse (most likely in their own minds) by fixating on all of the negatives of the situation and how it is making everything else worse, etc. While Josh never denied that possibility, he also did not fixate on that possibility. Rather, he used hindsight to begin owning up to his own mistakes, where things could have gone better on his end, and made plans on how he could better himself in the future.

Focus on What Can Go Right

This may sound a little too much like, "Focus on the bright side!" in terms of how to think, and while there are definitely elements of that mentality in this section, it does not go that far. Part of the problem with overthinkers is that they normally only focus on the negatives of life (it is pretty rare to find an overthinker who is positive, normally those are just incredibly hopeful optimists). Compared to overthinkers, who are predominantly negative, and hopeful optimists, who border on too positive, there is a happy middle ground.

Which is: focusing on what can go right.

Thankfully, this sounds exactly like what you are meant to do. Combatting overthinking is essentially everything you can possibly do to ensure that the negativity your brain is so used to producing is only produced when required. Including making the concentrated effort on noting when things can actually go right, or what you can do to make things go right. This can be something as simple as reminding yourself that it does not have to be that bad, that it may not actually be that bad, or that there is goodness in the world.

A great example would be to come up with one singular thing that you know is right and positive to begin combatting overthinking. For instance, say that your brain tends to overthink in the form of self-loathing, and the thought, "I suck at social interactions" is a common thought you have when things go wrong. You can focus on what can go right by battling that thought with, "I might be a bit awkward, but sometimes things go okay and I have a good time."

When it comes to focusing on what can go right, you

really need to start small. It is very, very easy to turn your overthinking brain into a brain that has latched onto toxic positivity, which then continues the cycle in a different way. Practice doing what the above example mentions, which is turning a negative overthinking pattern into an acknowledgement of the foundational truth, tacked on with a positive from past experiences. This will begin to help your brain notice when the overgeneralizations of your negative thought patterns have begun, validate your feelings of the overgeneralizations, and then begin to combat the negative overgeneralizations with known, true, positives.

The Right Perspective

Perspective is always key. It helps us understand other people, get to the bottom of our own feelings, and even help us begin to expect how some people will react or behave in certain situations. It is also key with overthinking, as it will start to force an overthinking brain to acknowledge where the overthinking has started and where that train of thought is wrong.

When we are on a negative spiral from overthinking, our brain is completely unaware; and frankly, no longer cares about the perspective for that scenario, comment, action, or thought, and how anything came about. It is simply following the mental path it has been building for a long time. Adding perspective can act like that big red "STOP" sign we see on the road. It causes overthinking to actually begin to stop, because the feelings and thoughts it is causing us to have are suddenly put into question.

Again, not in the way that those emotions are not valid, but rather into the question of whether those emotions are actually based off of the original triggering scenario. You have most likely noticed this yourself. When our brains are in overthinking mode, they are no longer fully aware of how things connect, because the negative spiral is a pre-existing mental pathway our brains have found loads of ways onto, and they do not really care how they get there. When you suddenly put perspective into the triggering event, you are able to give your brain a jolt out of its predetermined state and actually begin considering what it is thinking and why. It is pretty hard to continue beating yourself up mentally when perspective reminds your brain that you were originally upset about something completely unrelated.

Sometimes that jolt of reality is exactly what we need to implement the other good habits which have been discussed so far in this book, and it will certainly go a long way in helping you instill the other good habits that will be discussed in the upcoming chapters.

Now, here is the kicker—the perspective that you use has to be the right perspective; that does not mean right-wing, or the right answer. It has to be right as in, that was the reality of what has happened. This type of perspective is sometimes hard to remember or input because it is forcing our brain to remember a very recent traumatic or triggering event. However, there are many times where our overthinking brains need to be hit upside the head with a reality check (also known as perspective). Even if that reality is not pleasant, or is something we do not want to return to. Going back to the 'scene of the crime' as it were, in our minds, can provide numerous benefits. It can reinforce the facts (which our overthinking brains have probably ignored or skewed), it can remind us of why we were originally upset (or think of it as a reset to try and find an actual solution), and it can get us out of our negative mental downhill spiral.

Implementing this tactic to stop overthinking will be one of the harder things to do, because it will require a lot of mental honesty and transparency. Please note how that was not a green light to continue mentally beating yourself up. Even people who have long since gotten their overthinking under control still have a hard time implementing the right perspective in their minds. Why? Because this perspective is going to be so transparent with where we went wrong, what we did wrong, where we could have been better, or where we began to overthink. It is going to cause you to see, in real-time, your failures and vulnerabilities. Which is exactly where your overthinking comes in. Funny how one of the things we use to stop overthinking can actually be because of it as well. Just remember to do your best, and try to be self-aware of your thoughts and what caused them.

Being Aware of Your Emotions

This step is intricately tied to many parts of this book, but it was put in this chapter because being in tune with your emotions—including when you are overthinking—is a quick way to stop actually overthinking. Being aware of your emotions is also different from self-awareness, because this particular step requires that you are aware of what emotions caused you to spiral, and to accept them.

There you have it.

One of the biggest ways to combat your overthinking is not just to give new and positive thoughts to your brain, but also to accept the emotions which caused you to spiral out of control in the first place. Misplaced or ignored emotions bottle up inside of us, and how they come out is messy, harmful, and normally in a scenario which we openly admit did not deserve that type of outburst. While you may think that overthinking does not do that, as we now know, that is not always the case. Being aware of, and accepting every emotion you have will begin to stop that subconscious emotional bottle-and-explosion cycle that you most likely have on repeat.

Yes, it is very well acknowledged that this sounds way easier than it actually is. It is a lot of work to acknowledge and accept your emotions, because it requires that you actually think about why you are upset, and that is a path many of us do not want to go down. In all honesty, some of you may need professional help with this particular step, because it is so easy to believe that we have acknowledged and accepted our emotions when we really have not. It is only through the eyes of a professional or accountability partner who is really in tune with their own emotions who can tell the difference. Being aware of your emotions will go a long way in helping you combat overthinking, because you are going to start to get at the actual stem of why you overthink. It will force you to begin accepting and working on that past trauma, that past event or that reason, as to why overthinking is the solution your brain has come up with.

Journaling

So, the first question after reading this last section is, how many of you suddenly feel less of a desire to work on your overthinking minds, knowing all the work and specific emotional awareness it will require? Be honest.

There is no shame in seeing how much, and how hard, the work will actually be to combat overthinking and have moments of doubt, or an unwillingness to continue. Change is never easy, and it is guaranteed that those who have successfully gotten through it did doubt, stop, or want to stop, at one point in time. That is not a green light for you to actually stop, but acknowledging and helping you understand that you are not alone in wanting to (if you do) is not a bad thing either. We are all human, and sometimes the complicated emotions that go with that statement are just too much for us all the time.

So, take a break. Set a timer for five minutes and just let your mind wander. Make a cup of tea or coffee if you need to. But be sure to continue this book and to do the following journal prompts. Understanding yourself and implementing self awareness is hard. You are doing a fantastic job, and you can do this.

Out of all of the sections that have been discussed, which is the one that you are most keen to start right away? Pick that one, and then begin to write out one, small, daily actionable thing you can do from that segment in your daily routine to help begin building self-awareness.

How self-aware are you already? Where do you need to improve?

Were there parts of you that believe you may need more professional help with this section to combat your overthinking tendencies?

CHAPTER 5

Dump all Negative Thinking

Now that you have an understanding and the rudimentary conditioning on how to begin to stop overthinking, it is time to go onto the second step, which is to continue what was discussed in the previous chapter with a very specific goal: to dump all negative thinking and negative cycles.

It sounds almost too easy to be true (as has come to be one of the hallmarks of stopping overthinking), but halting your various types of negative spirals can do wonders for continuing to battle overthinking in the long run. As an overthinker, your brain is sadly already wired to be negative, which we saw when discussing the different manifestations of an overthinking brain. Obsessing, ruminating, worrying, and the cause of anxiety all combine towards negative mental habits. But then, what does this mean for your brain? Chances are you are already quite aware that this means your brain will begin to cycle down negative paths pretty quickly. Even the smallest slight or upset to your day, life, or scenario could trigger a negative mental spiral. Which is honestly most likely not something you are fully able to control, even if you are conscious of it. Your brain has become so accustomed to looking, implementing, and telling itself negative lies about itself, yourself, or life that it has become a really, really bad habit. One that you most likely cannot stop, even if you wanted to.

Yet, getting rid of, changing, altering, or replacing your mental negativity cycle is going to be one of your best paths to success; but it will also be the hardest. There is no sugar-coating this particular step, phase, or chapter. Battling and dumping your negativity cycle is going to most likely be one of the hardest things this book will prescribe for you. Let's face it; implementing everything which was discussed in the previous chapter is relatively easy to do right now because you are eager to start this journey. This book has ramped you up, and you are all set and ready to go. But what about when the momentum slows down, or you have an especially hard day? Or, what about when your brain will automatically begin a negativity cycle?

That is where due diligence, determination, and personal desire come in. All of which can be supplemented by beginning the habit of dumping all negative thinking.

The Negativity Cycle

The good news is that you are most likely aware of some of those spirals now, and may or may not have begun to analyze what triggered them and how your negativity particularly manifests itself. The fact that you are aware when you negatively spiral out of control and into deep bouts of depression, worrying, or whatever way your brain manifests overthinking, is a good thing (even though it really may not seem like it). Being aware is a good step, because this will allow you to begin taking hold of your thoughts and fighting them.

What is even better (in a manner of speaking) is that the negativity cycle is actually a very simple process of two steps. First, there is a triggering event, and second, your brain latches onto it and automatically begins to negatively spiral. The simplicity of the negativity cycle is a good thing, because there are actually less things for you to be aware of and combat. Even though they are incredibly hard, pervasive, and sneaky things, you only have two steps to be aware of and change.

So, then, what is the problem?

The problem is how easily your brain is now able to go into a negative spiral. Sure, there are definitely events, triggers, or scenarios where a negative spiral is actually really understandable and relatable. These things could be big life events like a massive breakup, a death, losing a job, or even moving to a new city and having to start all over. When our brains and bodies are overwhelmed, there is definitely a very, very strong urge to either be optimistic or negative. Not many people choose to be in the middle. Those scenarios—not that it is healthy to spiral out negatively—are almost easier to walk back out of, because the solutions to those spirals tend to be forced onto you; such as needing to find a new job, getting into a new relationship, healing yourself, or making friends and a new life in a new city.

But these types of events are most likely not what easily trigger you or someone you know into an overthinking negative mental spiral. Chances are, those triggers are actually tiny, little things, which to some people may be an innocent problem or a slight millisecond of frustration. Yet to an overthinking and negative brain, these events could be catastrophic. They could even be triggered by an innocent little negative thought like, "Oh, well isn't this just peachy?" (said with every inner frustration and sarcasm imaginable). It is really sad, and kind of scary, that this could actually be all it takes to convince your brain to begin a spiral into negativity: but there you have it. It is that easy. All it takes is that one particular moment, and everything positive which has actually happened to you that day becomes forgotten. Not that your brain would not acknowledge the positives of the day if it was reminded, but an overthinking brain on a negative spiral tends to forget those things exist until they are literally pushed to the forefront of the mind in an aggressive reminder.

Let's be honest, we have all been there, we have all had moments where those tiny little irritants are the one thing that wrecks our entire hour or maybe even day. The problem is that for an overthinking brain even this tiny little admission could potentially act like kryptonite for kick-starting your negativity cycle.

Why?

Coming full circle, the answer is because your brain is so accustomed to being negative. No, this does not mean you cannot validate any negativity you might be feeling, or that you need to create this fake and toxic form of positivity to stop the negative cycle. In order to actually dump and begin to combat your negativity cycle, you are going to have to exert a lot of self-control, self-awareness, and determination to get you through those tough moments.

Begin the Dump

This is where beginning to understand how to dump your negativity comes in. Essentially, what dumping your negativity looks like is a continuation of the cognitive replacement and heightening self-awareness suggestions from the previous chapter. According to the Calm Clinic, the steps to begin dumping all negative thoughts are as follows: installing and working on your awareness through identification and recording, finding the truth and analyzing your thoughts and feelings, disputing the negative thoughts, finding a positive replacement, and setting realistic goals (Abraham, 2022).

Small Note

Beginning to introduce cognitive replacement is tricky, and is not easily done alone. Be sure to keep someone in the loop during this stage, because the following steps could easily be overdone, become a replacement for negativity, introduce toxic positivity, or even become a new step in your brain's negativity cycle. That is not to say that you cannot do this alone, but if you are an extreme overthinker, even having a safe person who is aware of what you are attempting to help keep your mind clear and on the right track is highly recommended.

Identification and Recording

Awareness is the first step in beginning to dump your negative emotions. Creating the mental discipline and self-knowledge to be aware of your thoughts and feelings as they happen (for most of them, at least), will help you begin to identify when you are being negative and to spiral downwards.

The bad news is, just because you are aware does not necessarily mean that it will be any easier to stop your negative cycles. In fact, there may be a period of time where this is actually worse, because your brain is aware of what it is doing and what is happening, but your will and mind are still at war on what to do. You may be fighting the old habits of negativity with everything that has come up in this book so far, but your mind may not be completely accepting of these concepts.

For instance: Perhaps you have started to believe that you are actually really bad at a hobby you have been enjoying for the past few years. Even though you are technically aware of getting better, your negativity cycle has caused you to not believe the cold, hard truth through videos, photos, or even statements from your peers. Being aware when your brain is in a negativity cycle, which is causing you to believe the negative lies about yourself that your brain is feeding you, is a good start. Now you have to go a step deeper.

Being mentally aware of what is happening is not enough. It is great for the moment, or to jolt you out of the beginnings of a spiral momentarily, but you have to do more. Start with recording the entire moment. Whether it be in the journal used for this book, an app, or even a voice memo, you need to write down the scenario, your feelings, and your thoughts, to be able to gain perspective on the big picture rather than letting your brain continue to trick you with negativity.

What this does is begin to separate your feelings and thoughts from the actual problem, which is where a lot of people are able to begin problem solving. Which is what will be discussed in the following steps (Abraham, 2022).

Analyze

After writing down what caused your negativity, how it began to manifest, and the scenario behind it, it is time for you to actually re-read what you have written and begin to look for patterns in these events. Do you see any similarities in anything? Like in the event, what was said, how you responded, how you reacted, or how you became negative about yourself?

These similarities will point toward your own unique mental pattern, and finding this pattern will help increase your self-awareness with the goal of beginning to stop your negativity spirals more quickly, and to plant the seeds for finding solutions to these moments.

Find the Truth

Building off of your self analysis, you are finally ready to begin actually combatting the lies you are telling yourself. Remember: Just because your brain has gotten really good at lying to you, does not mean that what it is telling you during a negativity cycle is true. Which sounds really scary while reading it on paper. How weird, awful, and just icky to feel and know that your brain can lie to you; but it happens quite often, sadly. Think about that friend who dated yet another loser, even though you knew it was a bad idea, but they insisted that this person was a good change. Or when a friend or family member started to believe those specific pills were working. Our brains are so smart, yet can be so easily deceived. Which is why we have to begin building pillars of truth and understanding to combat everything our brain latches onto and somehow begins to believe is real. Including when your brain is having a grand old time lying to you in a negativity cycle.

Remember those negative, ruminating, obsessive, anxious, and worrying thought examples from earlier? Thoughts like: how much you sucked, how no one liked you, and how things would not get better? These are all lies your negative brain has decided are true.

It is now time for you to begin finding the truth in those lies.

You can do this by looking for cold, hard evidence to combat the lies your brain is telling yourself. Going back to our earlier example, this could be by looking at the recordings or photos of you performing your hobby to show how you are actually getting better. Or, to start asking your friends to record your improvements. There is nothing like going over your past and present videos to see progress and how things are getting better or going in the direction you want.

Other options are screenshotting positive messages from clients, friends, or peers, writing down body measurements, or even asking loved ones to record quick little messages you can keep on your phone about how they will always be there for you and love you.

The goal here is to have any kind of hard truth to prove to your brain that you are wrong.

Positive Replacement

This is where things can sometimes become a little tricky. Replacing a negative with a positive in your overthinking mental cycle is a good thing, but you have to be able to do it realistically. Lying to yourself, even if it is with a positive twist, or not allowing your negative emotions to be acknowledged and validated, is really just replacing a negative cycle with this incredibly whacked out positive cycle. Which is not what you want. Have you ever been in a stressful situation where you are definitely not really positive, but you somehow manage to go, "It's fine, it'll all be okay," with a positive voice, which, if we are being honest, was probably more sarcasm than actual fact? That is not what we are aiming for here.

Coming up with positive replacements is not going to be easy, especially since your brain is probably going to treat anything positive like a foreign object which must be destroyed. It is going to take a concentrated effort for you to introduce this particular step, but it is incredibly worth it and necessary for you to do. That being said, there are two main ways to begin implementing positive replacements in your mind. You can either begin replacing with a more neutral truth that acknowledges the negative but enables a positive potential, or insert forms of sincere gratitude.

Neutral Truth

When using the neutral truth method, you are essentially

replacing the blatant negativity of your mind by acknowledging the negativity and then bringing up an argument to stop the defeatism which is beginning to pop up.

For example: Perhaps you have begun to use negativity to isolate yourself from your social circles, with the lie that you did not enjoy yourself and no one wants you there. A neutral truth to the statement would be something like reminding yourself that you did have a good time while you were there, even though it took you a while to warm up to the atmosphere, and that your friends were glad you came.

In this example, you acknowledge that there were moments of awkwardness, but you began to reframe the context of your negativity by stating obvious facts, as well as memories and feelings that your brain is ignoring when pushing your negativity spiral. The truth you feed yourself is the actual truth, but it is neutral enough that your brain is able to tolerate its existence, while having the dual effect of beginning to stop the negative spiral.

The problem with neutral truths is that they can be easily

used to continue the negative spiral, rather than as the stopping force. When you enact this solution, you need to make sure that the neutral truths are strong enough to force your brain to stop being negative, even for a few minutes. Unfortunately, finding a universal example of this is a little tricky, since these neutral truths need to deal with you and that particular negative spiral; making the best way to use this method as a trial and error type of situation. The good news is, once you find the type of neutral truths that work for your brain, you will be able to easily employ them in the future.

Sincere Gratitude

Finding things to be grateful for can be a struggle, especially when we are not in a good place. Yet there is no denying that even acknowledging the simplest things to be grateful for, like: you are alive, you are breathing, the sun is shining, it is the perfect weather, etc., can go a long way in helping you reframe your mind (Lang, 2018). All you need is that one tiny thing. It may seem completely redundant or unnecessary, or may even seem really silly to be grateful for. But do not let that fool you. All you need is that one tiny little thing.

Here's the catch, though. This has to be real and sincere gratitude. It cannot be snarky, sarcastic, or based off of someone's ill-fortune or bad day. What you are grateful for has to solely do with you, and has to be something actually pleasant. The difference between these two things is often what messes people up when they attempt to employ this particular solution.

Being grateful that you are not the loser, or the one who is in worse shape, definitely has its benefits; but at the end of the day it is really like comparing two negatives and hoping for a positive. While that might work for math and algebraic problems, that is not how it works in the real world (most of the time; there may be the odd scenario which will be unique to you and what is happening around you). You need to be sincerely grateful for that one thing in your life, and that thing has to be something which is actually positive. The good news is that the sincerity and gratefulness you feel can be small at first. If you are out of practice in how to apply gratitude in your life, being one thousand percent, sincerely grateful, may feel fake, and almost like you are pushing too hard.

In this context, the sincerity we are looking for is the tiniest bit of relief you feel when you acknowledge that one thing in your day, week, month, year, or scenario has gone right. It could even be that you got to see a sunset on a really bad day.

Setting Realistic Goals

Setting realistic goals may seem like an odd thing to tack onto the end of explaining how to dump negativity, so here is the logic. Overthinking is a habit, and the goal of this book and overcoming your overthinking is to replace it with better and more productive habits for your brain and life. Just like when we are actually building a habit, replacing one follows the same guiding principles of consistency, taking small steps, and being realistic and understanding of yourself and your situations to ensure success.

Therefore, fighting your overthinking brain and dumping negativity with your own brand of realism, truth, and positivity, is going to require the exact same work as installing a new habit into your life. You already know how to do all of the other steps, and you most likely even know how to set a realistic goal. However, this section is more so a caution than an explanation.

Overthinking has designed your brain to constantly think poorly of yourself and your abilities. This can manifest in either making unrealistic expectations (perfectionism) and setting yourself up to fail, or not even trying because you are too afraid to (analysis paralysis). In either scenario, your ability and knowledge to begin setting realistic goals in your life, and, in how to insert and use neutral truths and positivity to combat your brain's instinct, will be crucial for being successful.

An example of a realistic goal in regards to dumping negativity could be that you want to spend the next month paying attention to neutral truths you could insert into negative spirals. This is a small, but drastic enough, step to help you start in the right direction.

Set yourself up for success. Start small, plan more, dream large.

The Actual Steps

Dumping your negativity cycle can also be called a brain dump, and it essentially will force you to take everything which is residing in your brain during an overthinking and negative cycle, and begin to tear them apart and confront them. In this section, we are going to summarize and put everything that has been discussed into actionable steps you can begin doing today, to start your journey on stopping overthinking. These steps are going to overlap with some of the previous sections, but thanks to the help of Ronald L. Banks, there are going to be a few twists and new steps added in (Banks, 2020).

Dump It

As with the above section, take everything in your brain and dump it somewhere physical. This could be a journal, voice memo, your phone, computer, tablet, whatever is easier for you. When you are dumping everything out, do not even try to sort or analyze what is going on. Just literally take every thought, emotion, and what is going on around and in you and put it on the page (Banks, 2020).

Sort It

Now comes the fun new stuff: Sort out every thought that you just wrote down. There are three categories you can put them into: general thoughts, actionable items, and emotions or feelings. Once you have written them down, read through them and begin to ask yourself what is actually important right now, or how much you will care about this later on. Asking yourself these questions will begin to bring in perspective and awareness, while also helping you acknowledge and feel your feelings without spiraling.

For instance, if you have a thought that says, "I am frustrated at this event," you read it and log it as an emotion, and then ask yourself how important that particular feeling is right now. You have the option of saying it is really important, or not really that important in hindsight. Either answer acknowledges the emotion, and will also begin to guide you on what to do about it (such as acting on the emotion or acknowledging it and then letting it go) (Banks, 2020).

Change Your View of Fear

Fear is something we steer away from, and sometimes that is a good thing. Fear is healthy, and it is a signal from our brain telling us when something is wrong, or needs to be avoided. Yet so often we use the tiniest bit of fear as a reason to not continue, or to not grow and change our boundaries, perspectives, or situations.

Think about it for a moment. Every new beginning you have ever had most likely had the tiniest bit of fear in it. Going to university, or college. Starting a new school. Starting a new job. Beginning that new relationship. Moving to a different apartment or town. Getting married. Entering a committed relationship. Every single one of these big moments probably had some fear in it. You most likely got through most of those situations okay. You fought that fear, won, and grew as a person. We need to stop avoiding all fear and discomfort, because it is in those areas where we see who we are and what we are capable of, and are where we grow. That is not to say we cannot acknowledge when we are uncomfortable, or adapt to make our fears easier to go through; the key is to acknowledge our fear, assess how dangerous it is, and if we should fight it (and in regards to overthinking, you really should) and then press onward.

We Cannot Predict the Future

Until science really catches up to some sci-fi movies, we are pretty much stuck admitting that we cannot predict the future (or at least, that most of us cannot, if you believe in that type of stuff). What this means for your overthinking brain is that every type of analysis paralysis and fear you feel in regards to the future is essentially just over-worrying, and is causing more stress and anxiety than you need.

Please note that this is not the same as evaluating the consequences of certain actions and making grounded decisions based off of those results.

What we are discussing here is you not doing something because you do not know if it will be a good outcome. Or, not changing because you are scared of what could happen. Being scared of the unknown is okay. Being scared of the future is okay. Letting the fear and lack of knowledge control you is not. Start to fight these fears by rationalizing through them. Journal your thoughts, your fears, and your true emotions. Acknowledge that if you want your future to be different, you have to look at the present and past you. What did you do to become who you are now? What do you need to change?

Stop Waiting for Perfection

As has been mentioned before, perfection is not always possible, and it has become a crutch. Wanting to be perfect, or waiting until everything is perfect, is a good way to let your overthinking brain win and to not change. Do not let it do that to you anymore. You are not going to like reading this, but nothing will ever be the level of perfection that you are waiting for to do whatever it is you need to do.

Control Your Emotions

Ah, so we are back at controlling our emotions. This is an incredibly tricky step, because it is going to require you actually battling your current emotions and thought patterns. Thankfully, as mentioned previously, controlling your emotions does not mean ignoring what you feel or why. It means you have to acknowledge your emotions and begin to come up with solutions to fix or solve them.

Visualize What Can Go Right

Another great word for this is 'manifesting.' Starting your day with a manifestation of what could go right in your day—and then finding a way to put these reminders directly in your face or visual sphere—for the rest of the day, will help combat your overthinking and negative mind. Yes, it really is that easy. By focusing on what could go right, you will be too busy retraining your brain to let overthinking latch on, or stay attached to your mental pathways of negativity.

Summary

Honestly, negativity sucks. It is absolutely awful and no fun in how it creeps into every part of our lives with no warning or care for what it is actually doing to our confidence, abilities, and even ways of life. What's worse is that our brain seems to naturally latch onto this negativity, even though it knows that this type of thinking is bad for us. It is so, so much easier to do than to constantly fight it.

But fighting it will bring you the life and the change you want. If you want to be successful in combating your overthinking, you need to start dumping the negativity in your life, particularly the negative spirals your overthinking tends to cause. Thankfully, negativity cycles are short and only have two steps, meaning that your ability to: analyze, find the truth, introduce positive replacement through neutral truths or sincere gratitude, and setting realistic goals, are perfectly within your grasp. You simply have to start.

Which is easier said than done.

Reminder

This entire book is written with the up-beat, positive vibes of encouragement to help you jump-start your actual journey in fighting overthinking. However, there is also the fine line between drinking the Kool-Aid of all the 'you can do it!' statements in this book, and understanding the fundamental fact that we are all human. It would be lovely if you could simply read this book and instantaneously fix and stop your overthinking. It is not that easy. You need to allow yourself to make mistakes, otherwise you are actually going to give your overthinking and negative brain a reason to not continue on this journey.

Now, is it for sure that you will fail on your first go-round? No. No one knows for certain, because it is up to you. This is merely a reminder that you need to give yourself the ability to be human and make mistakes, while also having the determination and follow-through to continue trying.

Journal

Alright, so, for this chapter take your journal and begin to think of ways that you can begin fighting and dumping your negativity.

Start off with trying to remember the last time you negatively spiraled (if you have not journaled one out already), and try to think of common elements to those spirals. What are the similarities?

Once you have those similarities, begin to analyze them and come up with truths you can use to combat them in the future.

Next, pick which type of positive replacement you want to start with first. Come up with a few reminders or gratitude-isms you can put either in a calendar, phone, or in your notebook to look at throughout the day and remind yourself of them before your negativity spirals out of control.

Then, begin to set realistic goals for yourself incorporating everything you have learned so far (this will also be repeated at the end of the book).

Finally, write down the 'why's' of why you want to do this. These reasons will be your reminder when the going gets tough, as well as help become a sort of progress marker. These 'why's' are really the reasons you are doing this, and the more you combat and overcome your overthinking, the more you will be able to answer and solve those 'why's.; Having a record of that will be incredibly rewarding, as well as become a new incentive to stick with it.

Chapter 6

Life-Changing Practices to Stop Overthinking

And at long last, it is time to start going over more daily practical ways you can start to stop your overthinking tendencies. This chapter will build on the principles, guidelines, and mental discussions we have had so far. Meaning, that it will be assumed you are already working on certain things, and what will be recommended for you here, will specifically discuss new and different techniques which will hopefully be able to work in sync with everything else so far. The key for each of these recommended practices is not only for you to be able to use them immediately, but for you to have options for every type of overthinking your brain decides to pursue. If one tactic does not work for you, try another; or if you know one tactic will work for one type of overthinking compared to another, utilize that to your advantage.

Regardless of where you are in your overthinking journey, these practices will be incredibly beneficial to you, and it is highly recommended that you start them immediately.

Practices to Stop Overthinking Forever

Down to business. Each of these sections will contain steps, tricks, and ideas on how to stop your overthinking brain, as well as building suggestions, and 'end goals.' These suggestions will be meant for you to return to once you have gained consistency within each individual practice. The 'end goals' are really just a picture of what this practice will look like in regards to you and your overthinking over a long period of time.

Pace Yourself

At the risk of sounding repetitive: The very first thing you should do is pace yourself. No, this is not a green light to stop reading this book, or to slow down the momentum you have been building while reading this book.

Instead, remember that change does not happen overnight. You are taking on a long and tiring endeavor, because you are now going to go toe-to-toe with yourself, which can be guaranteed to be a pretty heated and hard-earned victory when you win. Be strategic. No one knows yourself better than you, outside of maybe a parent or safe person (they will be more aware of your idiosyncrasies than you probably are, unless you are incredibly self-aware); meaning, that you are most likely already aware of any types of self-sabotaging behaviors you may try to use to stop this journey. Not because you do not want to change, but because this change is going to mean confronting past demons you may actually prefer to ignore, or that you are afraid of what will come.

Yes, you need, and should, fight that fear; but do it

wisely. Pace yourself. Set realistic goals, and let yourself be human and maybe fail (which, actually, is a great way to combat your overthinking brain, because you will be fighting your fear of change and confronting your need for perfection).

Pacing yourself is going to look different for everyone, so do not compare yourself to another person's journey. Use your newfound knowledge of awareness and cognitive replacement from the previous chapters to begin recognizing your self-sabotaging thoughts and to begin building actionable and realistic solutions to combat it.

Building

When it comes to pacing yourself, a great way to build on it is to actually continue on with it, and let it build with you. Sometimes, when we have paced ourselves for so long and then suddenly let go, our brains bounce back into this weird realm of, "Finally, I can go back to what I did before!" which is actually not what we want. Similar to implementing a new fitness routine or eating habit, pacing yourself can grow with you and your goals;

and this growth will feel relatively natural to you. Chances are, if you pace yourself correctly, you will not even realize when you have scaled it to meet your newfound growth.

End Goal

The end goal of pacing yourself is to build a newfound self-awareness of what you are capable of, and how you will be able to get there. Instead of either expecting to be perfect the first go-round, or to look at something and just say, "someday," and never have a plan to get there, you will have found that perfect middle ground. You know what you want, how to get there, and how to ensure that your brain and body stay consistent to accomplish that goal.

Solutions

Which brings us to the next practice you can incorporate: problem solving. Yes, sadly, that particular math problem from elementary school is actually a life trait we all need to be able to use. However, we are not going to ask you how many oranges Susie has if she left Tennessee at 60 miles per hour. Instead, we are going to get personal.

Ask yourself these questions:

- Why do you not solve some of your problems (the easy ones, not the traumatic or deep-rooted ones)?

- What is your natural tendency to solve problems, if your overthinking brain was not in the way?

- What is the one way other people solve problems that drives you absolutely nuts?

Now, look at your answers and see if there is a general pattern you recognize about yourself. It could be that you do not want to problem solve because you are terrified to do so, you do not want to get into a conflict based on past experiences, or you have done it too quickly in the past and it did not end well. Whatever your reason or pattern, it is time to begin confronting that, because your overthinking brain will actually begin to slow down if you confront its downward spiral with a solution.

So how do you actually find a solution?

Turn your problem into a question. Asking yourself a question is a great way to begin jump-starting or remind your brain that you actually need to solve this problem, while also beginning to perhaps have alternate forms of thinking start in your brain.

Utilizing this method will actually begin to work on several past actions we discussed, specifically: using the right perspective, inserting positive or neutral thoughts, and analyzing and sorting out your negativity and assigning it an action.

Building

As you build your solutions ability, you may not need to necessarily turn your problems into a question to begin thinking outside of the box. Again, this will most likely feel relatively more natural over time, because you will have trained your brain to look for actionable solutions rather than getting defeated or finding the solution which will not help you achieve what you want.

End Goal

The end goal of solution-making is to be able to take

your overthinking, break it down, and come up with healthy and actionable solutions to it.

Journaling

Journaling is a great way to begin gaining a new perspective on solutions. It is amazing how different things can seem when we are able to distance ourselves from our problems, thoughts, and emotions by putting them onto paper, a screen, or into a voice memo. In fact, you have most likely been utilizing this method throughout the entire book so far. So, now, take a moment and look back at your first journal entries to the one for the last chapter. How do you feel from all those different thoughts on paper? Are you still emotionally attached to them, or have you been able to distance yourself to find better ways to think?

Part of the reason we fixate so easily when we overthink is because there is nothing to stop us from noticing our actual thoughts and emotions. Our mind becomes this thing of its own, and it feels like we are just along for the ride. Journaling out your thoughts and emotions — especially while overthinking—will stop that.

It may not seem incredibly realistic to journal at the exact moment your brain starts to spiral out of control. What if it happens while you are in a meeting at work, or while you are in a fight with a loved one or colleague? You may not be able to journal right away, but since your brain is an overthinking brain, those thoughts and emotions are not going anywhere.

Begin to build the habit and discipline of bringing your journal with you everywhere, and make sure that you are able to find a quiet place to journal out your thoughts and feelings after the event, if you are unable to stop it immediately and begin journaling then. No matter when you journal out your problems, you are going to stop overthinking. Even if it is an hour or two after (although that is not ideal, but such is life).

The point of journaling is to remind your brain of the reality of the situation and to acknowledge your thoughts, but also to begin to distance yourself from them. This does not really have a time requirement, but this is also not the sign to journal only when you feel like it, when it is convenient, or to not journal altogether.

You may not like it, but you need something to distance yourself from your thoughts, and journaling will provide you with that ability.

Building

After journaling out your thoughts, as discussed in the previous chapter, you have a choice. You can either make actionable steps off of those emotions you are now re-reading, or you can ignore them. However, ignoring your feelings has to actually be because you are able and okay to ignore them. You cannot just simply disregard them because they are too much work or effort to deal with, or the actionable step they are pointing you towards is too much work (realistically, you can do that, but then you are not going to stop your overthinking patterns). Actionable steps are scary, and that is completely natural and normal to feel; but if you let that fear control you, then you are going to read this book and not be any different.

Similarly, you cannot use your journal as a crutch. Just because you journal and feel better does not mean that you can stop a conversation mid-way and journal right then and there. There are appropriate times and places to journal and put your feelings to paper, and you have to be aware of those.

Over time, you may realize that you do not need to journal as much as when you originally started this journey, because your brain has developed the ability of finding perspective within itself naturally and easily. This is actually possible, but it takes a lot of training and accountability to get there.

End Goal

The end goal of journaling—whether you actually keep this habit or not—is to help you find new ways to gain perspective and organize your thoughts as they come to you.

Meditation

Meditation is not just for yoga enthusiasts, it is for anyone who needs a moment and the space to breathe and distance themselves from their environments in a positive way. When it comes to overthinking, one of the best ways to meditate is to actually combine meditation, which is emptying your mind and focusing only on your breath, with mindfulness which is simply to just fixate on what you are doing. Nothing else. If you are folding laundry, just fold laundry. Do not let your brain begin to wander or think about all the negative things that it would like to, and do not fixate on the triggering event which caused the downward spiral. The key is to focus on the mundane and routine. This focus will stop your negative spiral, while also allowing those emotions to slowly drain out of you (also known as, you guessed it, gaining distance from your emotions to begin building your perspective).

Or, if that does not work for you, you can use the more yoga-esque way of meditating. Find a quiet place, sit still, and focus on your heartbeat and your breath. Slowly let your thoughts and emotions drain out of you, and only focus on your body. These actions will do the same thing as focusing on a mundane and routine task.

For the record, it is very well acknowledged how hard this is. Our overthinking brains are trained to think at top speed all the time, and our society and work lives have not made that any easier. Something is always happening, lists always need to be made, and emotions always need to be felt, validated, and acted on. Taking the time, energy, and even having the ability to let that all go and just focus on that one particular thing is going to be hard.

But you can do it.

Building

Building meditation really depends on what you are using it for, and how you do it. If you are using meditation to simply empty your mind to gain perspective, then you could build in such a way as to get to that place of blessed peace and neutrality more quickly. However, if you decide to tack on other things to meditation, such as using that as a quiet time to begin retraining your brain, or to implement new positive thoughts into your head, you could begin building or scaling how long you meditate per day, or how often.

End Goal

The end goal of meditation is different for everyone, because it has so many different benefits and possibilities. A great general end goal of meditation is being able to sink into that mindset easily and not be too worried about your surroundings or the necessary aids you needed previously to get there.

Distractions

This one may seem like a contradiction, considering that the last practice was about emptying your mind and only focusing on one thing to begin gaining perspective on your emotions. However, there are some days where that is honestly just not possible. Our thoughts, feelings, and emotions are this constant buzzing in the back of our heads that never goes away, like that annoying fly at a picnic.

If that is happening to you, find gentle and soothing distractions you can use to begin getting your brain to focus on anything other than the negative spiral it is insisting on. This could be something like: taking a hot shower, going for a walk, reading a book, listening to music, dancing, talking to a friend, or even going into nature. Anything that provides a physical or mental space to let your brain begin to calm down (Welle (www.dw.com), 2020).

The key with these distractions is that they distract you enough to gain distance from your overthinking, but not to the point where you forget and are unable to return to those thoughts. You may not really want to, but you need to return to these thoughts, because if they are nagging at you so badly where you are unable to meditate; your brain is most likely bringing to the surface something you actually need to pay attention to and address.

Building

Building this particular practice can go two ways. Either you are able to shorten the length of the distraction to gain perspective more quickly and bring about a resolution sooner, or, you are able to build this practice to the point where you address your overthinking with a calm or happy mind (depending on your situation).

End Goal

Honestly, the end goal for distracting yourself is actually to find the distraction(s) that work for you. There are going to be messy situations in this life, ones where we will need some type of self-soothing that is healthy and proactive, to help us find a place of peace and resolution. Finding one, or several, methods that you know will work for you, could do wonders as you go forward in life. In regards to overthinking, this practice will hopefully help you feel more capable in beginning to tackle and stop your overthinking tendencies.

Small Note

Remember way back in the introduction where we discussed the brain? Your environment is going to play a big factor in what you are able and willing to do when it comes to fighting your overthinking brain. This is especially important in this note because you are looking for healthy and peaceful distractions to help your brain distance itself from overthinking and begin to positively combat it. Being in a negative environment is not going to really help you proactively create that (if at all).

Pay special attention to your environment in regards to your distractions. If you pick a negative distraction (even if it is negative music) you may not notice the same positive effects you were aiming for.

If you are looking for ways to help this, here are a few quick tips (which are going to sound pretty similar to some other sections of this book, but bear with it for now). First, stop putting the wrong things in. This means being aware that something is negatively affecting you, and intentionally trying to stop using, going, or being there. Second, start putting the right thing in (or, begin to use positive replacement). Third, get the things that should not be there, out. Essentially, anything that is helping or continuing your negative mindsets should be addressed. If it is a relationship, ask the other person if they would be willing to attempt being more positive with you. If it is a workplace issue, begin to think about how you could make it more positive, or look for ways to change positions. If it is your living environment, begin to think of ways that you can safely make it more positive for you.

Yes, this is going to be a lot of work in and of itself, but it will be worth it. A positive environment will encourage a positive mindset, which will continue to encourage you to combat your overthinking tendencies.

However

If something is negative to the point where it is dangerous or toxic for you to be there, find a safe person to help you get out immediately.

Journal

Now that we are at the end of this book, begin to think about what you could actually start doing today, tomorrow, or this week.

Remember, Rome was not built in a day, and it is certainly not assumed that you will be able to beat your overthinking in a short timespan either, so let's just take that option right off the table. With time, diligence, and outside support through a mentor, safe person, or licensed therapist, you will be able to do this, but it will take time. So, now that you have been forced to acknowledge that this is going to be a long process, start to break down what you could do from this chapter immediately and how you are going to build on it.

So, which one of these practices do you think you could reasonably begin to incorporate daily?

How are you going to incorporate it?

How are you going to ensure that you continue to incorporate it when the going gets tough? (How are you going to stay accountable?)

Keep this journal with you as you begin to build and reach the end goal of these practices, return to these first day pages to see how you have scaled things and begun to figure out how your brain works. This type of personal insight will be invaluable in creating a healthier and stronger mind in combating your overthinking.

Conclusion

So we have come to the end of discussing how to combat your overthinking mind. We have gone over many things, so a few of the introductory things will be summarized and re-tied into the rest of what the book discussed, to help you begin to put everything together with a nice little metaphorical bow on top.

Overthinking is putting too much harmful thought into something. Even though our brain has fallen for the trap of believing this type of thinking is productive, it is not, and most likely never will be. When our brains overthink, they tend to concentrate on worrying, rumination, obsession, or anxiety-driven types of thoughts. Overthinking can present itself in two main ways: we are either worrying about the past, or are worrying about the future. We have continued to get away with this type of thinking because people have not called us out on it, we have convinced ourselves and everyone around us that it is productive thinking, or, we have done it for so long we are no longer fully aware of what we are doing. Regardless of how we got here, we are actively combatting brains that most likely have months, if not years, of ingrained negative behavior patterns.

These patterns are the habit of overthinking, which have to be replaced with new, positive habits. Remember: Nature abhors a vacuum, and getting rid of overthinking without putting something in its place would create a mental vacuum that we should not leave empty if our brain is ill-prepared to handle it. Without the proper hard work and determination, stopping overthinking will most likely just open your brain up to another bad habit, and we are back to where we started (but with a different book title).

Additionally, our habit of overthinking is most likely prompted and continued by living in a perpetual form of stress, which, in turn, has the potential to alter our brain's functionality and actual brain chemistry. Prolonged exposure to stress has potentially incredibly bad results for our brain; it can stop our fear center, as well as limit our brain's ability to learn, be social, and control the stress hormone of cortisol (TED-Ed, 2015).

But that is just what overthinking through stress does to our brains physically and chemically. When it comes to our actual mind, overthinking has a deeper and more problematic result. Remember: Our mind and our brain are two different parts of the same thing. Every thought we have enters our mind, which then begins to create neural pathways in our brain. These neural pathways encode every part of our thought, from the triggering action, to the actual thought, to our surrounding emotions and reactions. Additionally, the more those particular neural pathways are traveled, the stronger those pathways become. Meaning, that the more we continue down a negative mental path, the stronger those emotions and pathways become. When we consistently think negatively, like when we overthink, we are literally building stronger forms of negativity into our minds and brains through constant use of those neural pathways (Leaf, 2019).

Thankfully, your brain is able to bounce back and fix itself (TEDx Talks, 2020a). This is where all of the techniques and practices we have discussed come in. By finding ways to strengthen new neural pathways and replace old ones, you can overcome overthinking. However, you need to set yourself up for success. This includes being consistent, asking for help when you need it, and ensuring that you are allowing yourself to both succeed and fail.

While it may seem odd, if you do not allow yourself to have the potential to fail on this journey, you will actually fail. Why? Because putting in that mental wall of not letting yourself fail, you are actually continuing an overthinking tendency of perfectionism. Allowing yourself to fail is actively combatting that need for perfection while simultaneously giving yourself learning opportunities to find what ways work best for you in fighting your overthinking tendencies.

Also, remember that overthinking is not a form of

problem solving or self-reflection. Overthinking's inherent negative attitudes make sure that nothing productive comes out of those types of thoughts; meaning, that you will never be able to properly solve or reflect on anything when you are in that mental state.

By now you have hopefully been journaling for a few days and have begun to develop some introspective tendencies towards your overthinking brain and its peculiarities. Gaining these new insights about yourself may feel and seem defeating, but try to not let them get to you. You need to understand how your brain and overthinking is working in order to fully stop that particular habit, and this includes acknowledging some of the messy and not great sides to ourselves.

Just remember: Many people have been where you are, and have fought the same fight you are fighting. You are not alone in this, you are worthy of not thinking this way, and you are capable of doing it.

Also, do not be afraid or ashamed to reach out to someone, whether that be a safe person or a professional, to ask for help if you need to. Think of this journey like an elimination diet. It will be long, you may have a few tiny mess-ups, but hopefully, by the time you are finished with this journey, you will be more self-aware and able to tackle the things which caused you to stumble and mess up in the past.

You got this.

Thank You

Before you leave, I'd just like to say, thank you so much for purchasing my book.

I spent many days and nights working on this book so I could finally put this in your hands.

So, before you leave, I'd like to ask you a small favor.

Would you please consider posting a review on the platform? Your reviews are one of the best ways to support indie authors like me, and every review counts.

Your feedback will allow me to continue writing books just like this one, so let me know if you enjoyed it and why. I read every review and I would love to hear from you. To leave a review simply scan the QR code below or go to Amazon.com, go to "Your Orders" and then find it under "Digital Orders".

Scan the QR Code Below to Leave a Review:

Amazon US   Amazon Uk

References

Abraham, M. (2022, February 9). *Anxiety and Negative Thoughts.* Www.calmclinic.com. https://www.calmclinic.com/anxiety/symptoms/bad-thoughts

Acosta, K. (2022, January 11). *What Causes Overthinking—and 6 Ways To Stop.* Forbes Health. https://www.forbes.com/health/mind/what-causes-overthinking-and-6-ways-to-stop/

Alison. (2020, April 19). *How to Stop Overthinking and Relax - 7 Powerful Ideas.* Littleblogofpositivity.com. https://littleblogofpositivity.com/mental-wellbeing/how-to-stop-overthinking-7-powerful-ideas/

Banks, R. L. (2020, November 2). *7 Simple Ways to Help You to Stop Overthinking.* Www.youtube.com. https://www.youtube.com/watch?v=KO-hwqlGNCk

Cherry, K. (2021, February 1). *Why Toxic Positivity Can Be So Harmful.* Verywell Mind.

https://www.verywellmind.com/what-is-toxic-positivity-5093958

Cloud, H., & John Sims Townsend. (2004). *Boundaries*. Zondervan. (Original work published 2022)

Cloud, H., & John Sims Townsend. (2016). *Safe People: How to Find Relationships That Are Good for You and Avoid Those That Aren't*. Zondervan. (Original work published 2022)

Cuncic, A. (2020, July 1). *Change Your Thoughts, Reduce Your Social Anxiety*. Verywell Mind. https://www.verywellmind.com/what-is-cognitive-restructuring-3024490

Eliassen, R. (2016, August 30). *How to Stop Overthinking Everything | The Quickest Way!* Www.youtube.com. https://www.youtube.com/watch?v=EOsMDrT_X6I

Good Therapy. (2019, November 5). *Perfectionism*. Goodtherapy.org. https://www.goodtherapy.org/learn-about-therapy/issues/perfectionism

Koa Foundations. (n.d.). Koa Foundations | *How to Quit Overthinking Everything, Relax, and Move Forward*. Koa Foundations. Retrieved April 29, 2022, from https://foundations.koahealth.com/blog-post/how-to-stop-overthinking/

Lang, A. (2018). *The Beauty of Discomfort: How What We Avoid is What We Need*. Collins.

Leaf, C. (2019, April 17). How to Use Mind-Management to Rewrite & Redefine Your Life Story. Dr. Leaf. https://drleaf.com/blogs/news/how-to-use-mind-management-to-rewrite-redefine-your-life-story

Malin, J. (2021, May 21). *7 Clear Signs You're Overthinking Your Job*. Ladders | Business News & Career Advice. https://www.theladders.com/career-advice/7-clear-signs-youre-overthinking-your-job#:~:text=Usually%2C%20it

Merriam-Webster. (n.d.-a). *Obsession*. Www.merriam-Webster.com. Retrieved April 26, 2022, from https://www.merriam-webster.com/dictionary/obsession

Merriam-Webster. (n.d.-b). *Overthink*. Www.merriam-Webster.com. Retrieved April 19, 2022, from https://www.merriam-webster.com/dictionary/overthink

Merriam-Webster. (2019). *Anxiety*. Merriam-Webster.com. https://www.merriam-webster.com/dictionary/anxiety

Morin, A. (2019, January 7). *10 Signs You're an Overthinker*. Inc.com; Inc. https://www.inc.com/amy-morin/10-signs-you-think-too-much-and-what-you-can-do-about-it.html

Morin, A. (2020, April 20). *10 Signs You're Overthinking* (And What To Do About It). Forbes. https://www.forbes.com/sites/amymorin/2020/04/20/10-signs-youre-overthinking-and-what-to-do-about-it/?sh=17f033a92bb8

Parker-Pope, T. (2020, February 18). *How to Build Healthy Habits*. The New York Times. https://www.nytimes.com/2020/02/18/well/mind/how-to-build-healthy-habits.html

Relf, S. (2020, October 7). *Shut The F**k Up! - The Art of Managing Overthinking & Obsessive and Intrusive Thoughts*. Www.linkedin.com. https://www.linkedin.com/pulse/shut-fk-up-art-managing-overthinking-obsessive-intrusive-simon-relf/

References

Stein, M. (n.d.). *Why You Worry: Obsessing, Overthinking, and Overanalyzing Explained.* Www.effectivetherapysolutions.com. Retrieved April 22, 2022, from https://www.effectivetherapysolutions.com/anxiety/why-you-worry-obsessing-overthinking-and-overanalyzing-explained

TED-Ed. (2015). *How Stress Affects Your Brain* - Madhumita Murgia. In YouTube. https://www.youtube.com/watch?v=WuyPuH9ojCE

TEDx Talks. (2020a). *Science of Thought* | Caroline Leaf | TEDxOaksChristianSchool [YouTube Video]. In YouTube. https://www.youtube.com/watch?v=yjhANyrKpv8

TEDx Talks. (2020b, January 23). *How to Eliminate Self Doubt Forever & the Power of Your Unconscious Mind* | Peter Sage | TEDxPatras. Www.youtube.com. https://www.youtube.com/watch?v=v1ojZKWfShQ

Welle (www.dw.com), D. (2020, July 8). *Trick Your Brain to Stop Worrying and Overthinking* | DW | 07.08.2020. DW.COM. https://www.dw.com/en/trick-your-brain-to-stop-worrying-and-overthinking/a-54483817